WHEN THE SAI

WHEN THE SAINTS GO MARCHING

ON THE TRAIL OF COLUMBANUS

BARRY SLOAN

YOUCAXTON PUBLICATIONS

OXFORD & SHREWSBURY

Contents

For Elizabeth

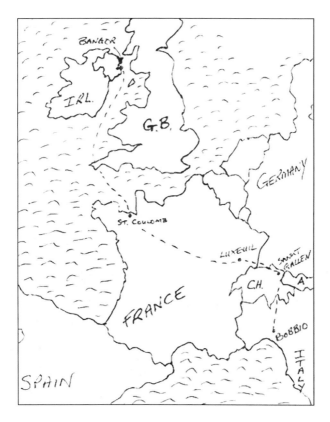

Main Sites on the Columban Way
from Bangor (Northern Ireland) to Bobbio (Italy)

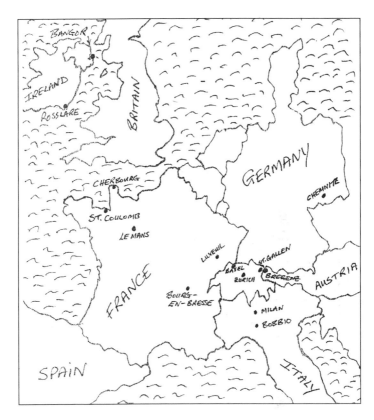

Places I Visited While Hitchhiking The Columban Way

Acknowledgments

I would like to thank all those who have been a blessing to me on this journey. Thank you to 'Miss Sophie' and 'James' - your love and support through the years has encouraged me more than you know. I am grateful to Marsden Fitzsimons for his advice in planning the route. Marsden, your list of VIPs was a Godsend. Fiona Orr and Sara Ann Swenson were the first to read my manuscript. Thank you, ladies, for all the constructive criticism, feedback and words of encouragement. My special thanks to the various European branches of "The Friends of Saint Columbanus" whose members welcomed, blessed and inspired me. Thanks also to my German publisher *Neukirchener-Verlag* who made the cover design available for the English edition. And, of course, a huge thank you to my wife, Gillian, whose love makes all things possible. You are my *Anam Cara*, my soulmate in the pilgrimage that is life.

Chapter 1

When the Saints Go Marching

I cannot remember a time when I have not been fascinated by the seaside town of Bangor. As a child I would often sit at my bedroom window and gaze out across Belfast Lough towards Bangor town. I spent hours with binoculars scouring its coastline, often wondering how far away it was. I wondered if you could swim across to it, dodging the cargo ships and passenger ferries that made their way up Belfast Lough on their onward journey to Scotland, Liverpool or the Isle of Man.

As a teenager I discovered that it is approximately five miles to Bangor, as the crow flies, or rather as the fish swims, and that you actually can swim this stretch of water—if you are mad enough—like one of my friends. Tommy swam from my home town Carrickfergus across the Lough to Bangor one summer's day. Just for a dare. He managed the five mile stretch, safely negotiating the shipping lanes, but was so knackered when he reached Bangor that he had no strength to swim back home again.

Unfortunately Tommy had not been bright enough to consider this scenario before accepting the challenge of his peers, and so here he was, stranded at the other side of the lough wearing nothing but a pair of speedos. With no money, no phone—mobiles had yet to be invented—and no way of letting anyone know where he was, his only option was to go to the police station and ask for help.

I can't imagine what the local Royal Ulster Constabulary officers thought when they looked through the darkened reinforced glass windows of their police barracks only to see *Speedoman* approaching. A bizarre scene for sure—maybe a bit like one of those conundrums you try to solve with your mates in the pub: a man with a backpack is found dead, lying facedown in the desert, miles away from civilization. Explain.

Maybe the strange sight of *Speedoman* brought out the detective in those bemused constables. Perhaps this incident is even used today as a case study in the training of young recruits: a young man wearing nothing but bright red swimming trunks, still wet, cautiously approaches your roadside checkpoint—what action do you take? Please tick as appropriate:

- ask to see his driving license
- tell him to empty his pockets
- do a breathalyzer test
- arrest him for indecent exposure
- ask him if he has just swum across Belfast Lough

Of course, it could be none of the above. The man could simply be a victim of a mugging. Admittedly, the muggers would need to have been quite desperate to take almost all his clothes. And then again a mugging doesn't really account for the wet swimming trunks, unless that is, they had to water-board the victim (who by the way just happened to prefer swimming trunks to boxers), in order to get the pin number of his credit card? Desperate muggers indeed.

Or maybe those budding young police recruits in training would suggest something completely different. It could for instance be terrorist related—don't forget this was Northern Ireland in the 1970's. Perhaps a new tactic of the IRA? (Please note: I am choosing here to ignore any was-he-packing-a-weapon jokes.) But what tactic could there be in sending a young man wearing nothing but swimming trunks to a heavily fortified police station in a busy town centre? Let's face it—he is unlikely to be a suicide bomber concealing a load of explosives on his person.

No, the only logic I can find in any so-called terrorist swimwear tactics would be to distract police officers in their course of duty, which pretty much sums up what *Speedoman* did that day when he revealed all—well, not quite all, but you know what I mean. Two officers drove him back home to Carrickfergus, forty-five minutes by car, just long enough for a lecture about not wasting police time, and to tell the young Tommy to get a life.

The only time I went to Bangor as a child was on Easter Tuesday. In fact I was in Bangor on Easter Tuesday for about five years in a row, because it was the venue for the annual Easter parade of the Junior Orange Order. This organisation, with its annual parades celebrating Protestant culture and religion, was—and still is—an important part of life for many in my community. As a member of LOL 52, I always looked forward to Easter Tuesday, when I would wear my new white shirt, crimson-coloured lodge tie and white gloves, along with the orange sash, clearly identifying me as a member of Loyal Orange Lodge number 52. I was only 10 years old but felt much older, marching with my tribe to the beat of the drum around our housing estate before traveling by bus to

Bangor, where we joined dozens of other lodges and bands for the main parade.

I looked forward to marching to 'the field' behind our flute band which prided itself in being louder and rowdier than the other so-called 'blood and thunder' bands. (Truth is, these bands were actually more often thud and blunder.) I looked forward to the crowds of onlookers who always commented on "how well the boys look today"; to my cousin's hamburger stall at the field, where I got free drinks with my burger—it obviously didn't hurt him too much, seeing that he's a millionaire businessman in Belfast today; to the tuppenny falls in the amusement arcade in the town; to buying a present for my wee brother—usually a stick of Bangor rock; and to finishing eating my fish and chips on the bus home, before we reached a certain section of north Belfast, where our bus was usually pelted with stones by kids from the 'other side'.

These kids, I might add, probably knew as little about why they were throwing stones at us, as we knew about why we were marching in Bangor. Pretty naive. I guess we were all quite green back then.

Thirty-five years later I am once again heading to the town of Bangor, and once again for religious reasons. This time however I march to the beat of a different drum, so to speak. Having experienced my own personal 'reformation', I now understand what it actually means to be "Protestant". No longer is it a term that determines which side of the sectarian divide a person in Northern Ireland is supposed to belong to. Nor is it a term that automatically defines where someone's political affinities lie. For me today, being a Protestant has to do with being a practising Christian. It's about professing a living faith in a God who walked this earth breaking down every conceivable barrier and crossing all borders in order to reach people with life-changing love.

I head to Bangor as an ordained Methodist minister, and as a missionary who has been living and serving in Chemnitz in the eastern part of Germany for the past thirteen years. My Northern Irish roots along with my connection to Germany make my trip to Bangor today all the more poignant. Today I begin a journey in the footsteps of that small group of Irish monks who in the late sixth century set out as missionaries from Bangor to continental Europe. These twelve missionary monks, along with their charismatic leader, Columbanus, brought the gospel once again to among others the German-speaking people of their day. This is what makes the story of the Bangor monks so fascinating for me. I live, work and minister in Germany today. The fact that my fellow Irishmen have already been there, done that and got the proverbial T-shirt—fourteen hundred years ago into the bargain—makes me want to retrace their footsteps today.

This trip, which will take me to France, Germany, Switzerland, Austria and Italy, is a first for me. For a start, it's my first ever sabbatical—a three month break from the demands of ministry for renewal, relaxation, and re-charging the batteries. It's also a first for me because I plan to walk and hitchhike the route as much as possible. I could travel in comfort by car or by train and stay in hotels along the way, but that is not really what this journey is about for me. Whether or not it's the first signs of an approaching midlife crisis, I find the idea of backpacking and hitchhiking through Europe quite appealing.

The route that I will take on my Columban adventure is not a recognized pilgrim route like the famous Camino de Santiago (Way of St. James), which leads to the cathedral of Santiago de Compostela in northern Spain, where the Apostle James is supposedly buried. On my route there will be no official pilgrim guest houses and no helpful road signs clearly directing the way. My plan is simply to concentrate on visiting the main monastic centres that were established in Europe by Columbanus and his disciples. These are to be found in Saint Coulomb and Luxeuil (both in France), Saint Gallen (Switzerland), Bregenz (Austria) and Bobbio (Italy).

The actual route I take to reach these destinations is not important to me, and will most likely be determined by the hitchhiking options available to me en route. I am happy to just go with the flow and see what happens. With any luck it will not be as nerve-wracking as the time I drove through a war zone in Croatia shortly after the Balkan wars when all the road signs had been removed and I ended up working out my route from the position of the sun in the sky. At least this time I don't have a wife and two small kids in the car with me.

Hitchhiking is also a great way to meet people and get a better understanding of the different regions and cultures. I love meeting new people. It's one of my hobbies. That's why, whenever possible, I stop to pick up hikers in my car. When I was living and ministering in County Fermanagh on the border to the Republic of Ireland and needed to travel back up to Belfast for an appointment, I would often leave my car at home and thumb a lift, just so that I could meet new people.

The Bangor monks of the sixth century had the practice of always walking because this made it easier for them to meet people and share the gospel with them. Walking brought the missionary closer to the people he was trying to reach. I suppose hitchhiking could be seen as the modern day equivalent. At least I have a captive audience in a car!

I have never hitchhiked on continental Europe, however. Nor have I ever travelled not knowing exactly where I was heading, or if I would even have a bed for the night. This is definitely a first for me, but I am excited at the prospect. I see myself as a kind of modern day pilgrim, traveling in the spirit of those early Irish monks, who left behind all worldly possessions, stepped outside their comfort zone and depended solely on the providence of God for each day's daily bread. Yes, the romance of it all appeals to me. Nevertheless, I decide to bring two credit cards and my iPhone with me, just in case. Doubting God's providence is, alas, not a first for me.

There is, however, one further reason why this journey is a first for me. This is my first excursion into the history of the Bangor monks of the early Middle Ages who transformed the religious and cultural landscape of much of Europe. In my church history studies at theological seminary I had looked in depth at the history of the early church; from the book of the Acts of the Apostles through to the conversion of the Roman Emperor, Constantine. It was during Constantine's reign at the start of the 4th century that Christianity became the official religion of the Roman empire. It's fascinating stuff about the spread of Christianity in the face of apparently insurmountable problems like heresy, heathenism and fierce systemic persecution.

I also learned about Saint Patrick and the beginnings of Christianity in fifth century Ireland. Saint Patrick is probably known first and foremost today for the legend that tells of him banishing the snakes from Ireland, which contrary to popular belief, has nothing to do with actual snakes. The banishing of snakes refers to Patrick ridding Ireland of pagans—pagan devils, as the celtic Christians called them, symbolized by snakes.

Nevertheless, I still think of real snakes, when I remember the question with which my dear old professor of church history began his course on Saint Patrick, "What did Saint Patrick say to the snakes as he was driving them out of Ireland?" After allowing his students a few seconds to consider the answer, my professor, with a mischievous twinkle in his eye, would then look over his shoulder, mimic holding a steering wheel, and say, "Are you alright in the back there, lads?" Not a bad way to start a course, if you ask me. The old boy certainly had our attention for the important stuff he then went on to teach us.

I also thoroughly enjoyed my church history modules on the Reformation, of course without at that time knowing that I myself would later be ministering in Germany, in Saxony-Anhalt, the very state where in 1512 an Augustine Monk named Martin Luther nailed his ninety-five thesis to the door of a church, beginning a process which eventually led to the Reformation and the creation of the Protestant church.

Training for the ordained ministry in the Methodist Church of Ireland I could not fail to cover eighteenth century church history because of its significance for the rise of Methodism and its renewing impact on the Church in the British Isles. The Methodists, with their dual focus on social justice and spiritual renewal, brought balance back to a church that had mostly lost its way, ensuring once again a true religion of hand and heart, word and deed.

Yes, I can safely say I found church history fascinating, and thoroughly enjoyed my studies. But I had never studied the medieval period. In place of medieval church history I opted instead for 'Early Christian Doctrines', and so I ended up dealing with heresies like donatism (don't ask), gnosticism (google it) and a few other 'isms', (theologians love their 'isms'), when I could have been busying myself with the Indiana-Jones-like missionary adventures of Columbanus, Gallus and those other monks from Bangor.

There was, however, another factor that had contributed to my ignorance of the Bangor missionaries of the 6th century. Sainthood. Not mine, obviously. Let me explain. Saints on the whole are not high up on the agenda in the Protestant mindset. Put another way, saints tend to be a Roman Catholic thing, or at least not a free-church thing, which a lot of Protestant churches are, including the Methodist Church in which I minister.

The average two dimensional Protestant growing up in Northern Ireland, where politics and religion have always been uneasy bedfellows, is oblivious to many important and significant parts of his national Christian heritage, simply because he considers it to be Catholic, Irish (i.e. not British), or worse. Hence, anyone whose name is prefixed with the word "saint" is considered suspect. Yes, even good old Saint Patrick is still too Roman Catholic for some Northern Ireland so-called Protestants, so you can probably imagine what they think, when they hear names like Saint Comgall, Saint Columbanus or Saint Gall. To the untrained Protestant ear, it just sounds too Catholic, too papist, even if these guys were all from Bangor, ironically a predominantly Protestant town today.

I must confess that I recognize some of this ill-informed, narrow-mindedness in my own upbringing. I am a child of my time, a time in Northern Ireland when Protestants and Catholics attended different schools, segregated on religious grounds; a time when fear and mistrust on both sides of the religious divide ploughed the soil for seeds of hate and sectarianism; a time when the past meant more than the future; a time when politics was tribal and religion was man-made, often with no real room for God and good. Growing up on a Protestant working class housing estate in Carrickfergus, I neither had the opportunity, nor the inclination, to get excited about some obscure medieval saints with Catholic-sounding names.

But today, all this changes. Today I am very much excited about getting to know these giants of mission, these unsung heroes of Ulster. It is time to fill in all the blanks, to join up all the dots. It is time to see the whole picture—saints and all.

I can't wait to discover what God wants to say to me through these ancient Irish spiritual ancestors of mine; what they can teach me about life, about faith, and about combining the two in meaningful, relevant ways, that might just make the world a better place. On this journey with medieval saints, I look forward to being surprised by the modern day ones I meet along the way.

I am also hoping this journey of discovery in the footsteps of Saint Columbanus and his twelve missionary companions from Bangor will shed light on my own dark ages, my own dark edges, offering explanations to some of the stuff that is currently puzzling me—deep stuff, heavy stuff, God stuff, life stuff. Stuff much more complicated than the case of the man with a backpack lying facedown, dead in the desert ... whose parachute simply failed to open. Who knows? Maybe the answers are staring us in the face.

Chapter 2

Bangor Boats Away

I decide to travel the short journey from Belfast to Bangor by train. Leaving Central Station we pass the Odyssey, home of the Belfast Giants, Northern Ireland's only professional ice hockey team. Less than a mile further down the line are some of Ulster's other giants: the iconic cranes dominating Belfast's skyline that belong to Harland and Wolff, once the world's largest shipyard and birthplace of the Titanic (she was alright when she left here!), and the George Best City Airport, named after the local lad who became one of the world's greatest footballers (If you don't believe me, ask Brazil's Pele!). Bangor bound, the train continues, passing luxury homes and fashionable small towns hugging the shoreline of the aptly named Gold Coast of Belfast Lough.

It's not difficult to understand why you would want to settle here. Apparently Saint Patrick was of the same opinion. According to legend, Patrick and his companions came one day to a certain valley to rest. Suddenly the valley was illuminated with a host of angels and a celestial choir singing God's praise. Patrick named the place "Vallis Angelorum", and in due time, here in this "Valley of the Angels", a holy place would be built that would lead to Ireland later being called the "land of saints and scholars". That holy place was Bangor, a monastic community founded by Saint Comgall in 558 AD.

Gazing out of the train window, my thoughts drift back to some of the things I had been reading in Thomas Cahill's brilliant book, *How the Irish Saved Civilization*, in preparation for my Columban adventure. Only then could I understand why Columbanus and those other Bangor monks were able to do the hardest thing an Irishman could ever do—a thing much harder even than giving up his life—leave Ireland. I was fascinated to learn how the missionary monks of Ireland were able to found monasteries that in time would become the European cities of Auxerre, Luxeuil, Bobbio, Würzburg, Regensburg, Saint Gallen and Vienna, to name but a few. The Roman empire—or lack of it in Ireland—and its fall, play significant roles in this story. The details are fascinating.

Julius Caesar invaded Britain in 55 BC, extending Rome's empire to the western edges of Europe. By AD 82 Gnaeus Julius Agricola, then governor of Britain and in command of the XX Legion and the Irish Sea flotilla, was ready to set sail for Ulster in order to conquer this island (Hibernia) for the empire. However, it was never to be. A legion of German conscripts stationed in Galloway mutinied, forcing Roman Emperor Domitian to order his governor north to quell the disturbances. By the time Governor Agricola returned, the cracks in the Roman empire were beginning to show, and the Romans were now forced to retreat behind Hadrian's wall, with other matters to occupy them rather than an invasion of Ulster.

Thanks to the Germans, Ireland remained unconquered by the Romans, and as a result we had to wait another nineteen hundred years for decent straight roads!

In the fourth and fifth centuries the Roman empire was facing attack from German-speaking peoples from central and northern Europe. This led to more and more legions being withdrawn from the outposts of the empire to defend Rome, leaving Roman Britain prey to barbarian invaders. The Picts attacked from the north, the English from the east, and the Irish from the west. The raiding Irish tribes brought back treasures or captives from Roman Britain to Ireland, one of them being a young man called Patricius (Patrick), who along with others would ensure that if the Roman empire did not reach Ireland, at least its religion would.

As a slave, Patrick tended sheep for six years in the area known today as County Antrim in Northern Ireland. Facing constant coldness and hunger, he was comforted and strengthened by his Christian faith, until he was finally able to escape on a pirate ship and return to his native Britain. God, who obviously has a sense of humour, then appeared to Patrick in a vision, calling him back to Ireland, this time as a missionary, bringing the Christian faith to his one-time captors. When I see how the two sides of the religious divide in Northern Ireland fight over Saint Patrick and whose side he would be on today, I despair. I can't help thinking how great it would be if more Ulster people experienced and lived out their faith the way Patrick did—a faith that enables one not only to move on from the past, but to actually go back and serve the ones who caused you so much hurt in the past. Now that's what I call conversion!

Taking holy orders, Patrick evangelized Ulster around the middle of the fifth century, being particularly successful among the ruling class. These local gaelic kings—there were hundreds of them—would often donate land to the church and become patrons of the new monasteries that were now springing up all over Ireland. One such monastic site was Bangor, on the north eastern coast of the island.

As so often was the case, the place, that would later become a town or city, started as a monastic site with a few monks living in simple beehive huts around a modest church sanctuary, and other buildings used for farming or handcrafts, wash-houses or guest houses. As there were no villages or towns in Ireland until the ninth century, the monastic sites became the religious, cultural and economic centres of Ireland. Bangor was no exception. As a centre of learning and Christian witness in the sixth century, Bangor was rivaled perhaps only by Iona which was founded by that other great Irish pioneer missionary, Saint Columcille of Derry.

I am abruptly pulled back into the twenty-first century by a group of teenagers who have begun terrorizing the whole train carriage with their foul language and anti-social behaviour. Alas, the land of saints and scholars is obviously not without its sinners and simpletons. As the train pulls into Bangor station I observe these youngsters, with their fifty quid football tops and the latest smart phones, leave a trail of chaos in their wake. Disembarking the train, I quietly offer up a prayer for them, for their parents, and indeed for myself, that God will continually help us to recognize that the important things in life are not things.

I exit the train station and walk up Abbey Street, struggling to overcome the temptations all around me—Fish 'n Chip shops. One of the downsides of living in Germany is that you are in the land that the chippy-god forgot, which is why

I usually over-compensate when I am visiting family back home in Northern Ireland. In a moment of weakness I stop outside *Captain Cod* and torment myself, dreaming about pastie suppers and battered onion rings with loads of salt and vinegar. The flesh is willing, but thankfully the Spirit is not weak, and I am soon on my way again, with the spiritual home of Columbanus in my sights, just a few hundred yards up the road ahead of me.

The first thing that strikes me about Bangor Abbey is its historic graveyard. I have been living in Germany for the past thirteen years and I had forgotten how old Irish graves and gravestones can be. There are some permanent graves in Germany, but the vast majority of graves are temporary, and are 'cleared' and made ready for re-use after as little as twenty years, when all human remains have (presumably?) fully decomposed.

I have often wondered how they know when exactly the remains are fully decomposed. Do they do tests? Do they have to take soil samples every year? Is the biological breakdown of human bodies an exact science with proven formulae that determine exactly how long any given mass of human matter takes to decompose? Does $D = T \times M$, where D is Decomposition, T is time, and M is mass. What about really large people? Is there a difference? And what about the clothing the deceased are wearing when they are buried? Some of those synthetics would surely take millennia to decompose.

The whole thing baffles me. Just like when I first walked around a German cemetery, and noticed that everyone buried there had passed away within the last twenty years. Why did nobody die before this, I wondered. Perhaps it was just this particular graveyard that was only twenty years old? No, I visited other cemeteries and I found it totally bizarre that every single person that was buried there had also died within the last twenty years! Where were the all the others buried? Had I lost the plot completely? Had I lost millions of them?

Maybe the German system of re-using burial plots has something to do with the fact that there are eighty million Germans. After all, only six million people inhabit the whole island of Ireland—we obviously have much more space. I am sure things would look different for us, if we had burial plots for cows.

However, the more I think about it, the more I am convinced that it probably has more to do with the renowned German sense of orderliness and exactness. Their cemeteries are meticulously cared for, and kept in perfect condition, which is why I just don't think the German psyche could cope with overgrown cemeteries with rows of higgelty-piggelty, lopsided, illegible headstones.

The historic graveyard in Bangor Abbey—I say graveyard because 'cemetery' just sounds too modern in this instance—is definitely not German. The grass is long, short, uncut or partly cut, neat and wild, depending on where you are standing; and the headstones are on the whole definitely more than twenty years old. In fact some of them even go back to the eighteenth century, which accounts for them leaning, sinking or generally exhibiting the effects of three hundred years of Ulster wind and rain, not to mention the roughly one hundred hazardous years since the introduction of the lawnmower.

This is a special place. Like any cemetery, it is a holy place, a place full of history, each headstone telling its own story, each grave bearing a loved one, one loved by God. I take my time, walking respectfully among the graves, crosses and headstones pausing to decipher some of the old English script on the weather-beaten slabs. I am moved by a verse on a tombstone of a young sailor who drowned off the coast of Jamaica in 1829, aged 25:

"But oh there was hope in that dear sailor's death;
For in youth he had learned his Redeemer to love.
On that Saviour he called with his last parting breath;
To receive him in peace to the mansions above."

The verse, chosen by this young man's parents, speaks of hope in the face of death, a central and powerful tenet of the Christian faith. As a pastor I have officiated at many funerals myself, and I know how helpful and comforting such words are to a believer. They can quite literally be the difference between life and death.

The fact that the first Christians in Ireland were well aware of this meant that more and more hungry souls were finding faith in the risen Christ, and beginning life anew. One such hungry soul was a soldier from Magheramourne in County Antrim who converted to Christianity and was later ordained deacon and priest. His name was Comgall, the founding abbot of Bangor Abbey.

Comgall gathered a band of monks around him in Bangor whose saintly lives and scholarly attainments became the wonder of their age. By the time of his death in 602 AD, Saint Comgall had charge over 3000 monks, and Bangor Mór, "the great Bangor", was one of the leading lights of celtic Christianity. (Note to Northern Ireland Protestants: Relax. Celtic is simply a historical term and in this context has nothing whatsoever to do with a football team from Glasgow.) For almost three hundred years Bangor Abbey would be one of the most important monastic schools in Europe.

Monastic life under Comgall was hard, characterised by his strict rule of prayer and fasting. Although, either the prayers were more effective or the fasting was less extreme, because this time no monks died, which was not the case with Comgall's last monastic community on Lough Erne where seven monks died due to the severity of his monastic disciplines! Nevertheless, the monks' food in Bangor was scant and plain, with milk even being considered an indulgence. The monks had one meal a day, taken in the evening and eaten in silence. Come to think of it, if they'd had pastie suppers and battered onion rings in those days, they may never have left Bangor at all.

The worship services were central to the life of the community. There were five held during the day and three at night, and all were scrupulously observed. This brings new perspective to my complaining about the early start to church services in Germany. When I first came to minister in Germany, one of my churches held its Sunday worship service at eight-thirty in the morning. In Northern Ireland I was used to church starting at eleven o'clock or even eleven-thirty. That was why I was only half-joking when I referred to that particular German church service as the night shift.

I know that a lot of people are early birds, bright and chirpy from the crack of dawn, but I am not one of them. My own voice is not usually even recognizable as human until around 10 am, which is why I never cease to be amazed at how well we sing at church, yes even at the eight-thirty service.

Maybe one explanation is the simple fact that Germans, and especially east Germans, start the day a lot earlier than we do in Northern Ireland. I discovered this in my very first week in east Germany when I was wakened at 6.30am by someone ringing our apartment doorbell. I was sure it was some kind of emergency, an accident that had just occurred and I was needed at the hospital; or someone was dying and the family wanted their pastor at the bedside of their loved one. Even the sight of a fireman calling to evacuate the building would not have surprised me as much as what happened next. Still half asleep, wearing only boxers and a T-shirt, I opened the door to be greeted by the local plumber who had come to plumb in our washing machine. At 6.30am! You could have knocked me over with a tap wrench.

Even if my new parish in Germany meant that I had a worship service that began at 8.30am, at least, unlike the Bangor monks, I did not have five services per day, with an additional three at night. Reminding myself that everything is relative, I am thankful and decide in future not to moan about my 'night shifts'.

The worship life of the Bangor monks was not only characterised by an above average number of daily devotions and divine worship services, but more especially by their quality and their intensity. In short, devotions in Comgall's day were dense and intense. Bangor was famous for its music and its antiphonal singing, which was a kind of responsive singing, where some monks would sing a verse or phrase and other monks would then sing a response or reply. This ministry of singing continued around the clock, each choir being replaced by the next choir without intermission, so that the singing never ceased all year round.

Some of the hymns, prayers, and anthems that were sung at Bangor have been preserved in a Psalter, a hymn book known as the Bangor Antiphonary, dated at around 680 AD. This early 'mission praise' book of prayers and songs was probably carried from Bangor to Bobbio in Italy in the ninth century in order to avoid its destruction by the Vikings, who at that time were plundering Ulster. It is currently held in the Ambrosian Library in Milan (Note to football fans—not far from the San Siro Stadium).

Proceeding through the main entrance to the Abbey, I am met by two kind and helpful retired ladies, volunteer tour guides, who welcome me and endeavour to answer my many questions. The original monastery of Comgall's time is sadly no longer standing, having been ransacked on numerous occasions by the Vikings in the eighth and ninth centuries. The present day abbey was restored in 1617, although parts of the building date back as far as the twelfth century. Hanging in the foyer is a complete record of abbots and rectors who have served the abbey up until nineteen-sixty. It is truly remarkable—from the founding days of Comgall, to its times as an Augustinian and Franciscan monastery, to the reformation, when the Abbey became a Protestant church.

Standing at the back of the church and looking past the choir stalls into the chancel (altar area), I catch my first glimpse of the Bangor saints painted onto the "east wall" (the wall in churches behind the chancel—even if it does not face east, which by the way it does in Bangor Abbey). It is a dramatic painting of the ascension of Christ into heaven, witnessed by Comgall, Columbanus and Gall, the three servants of Christ whose missionary spirit so dramatically changed the course of European history.

It is exactly this missionary spirit of Bangor that so interests me. Columbanus and Gall were sent out from Bangor as missionaries in the sixth century to bring the gospel of God's love to, among others, the *Alemanni*, the Germans. Today, fourteen hundred years later, yours truly, another missionary, or as it is more accurately termed in the Methodist Church, a mission partner, is also working in the German mission field. I am a mission partner, a partner in mission. The word 'partner' emphasises a joint and equal respect, a two-way relationship, a giving and receiving in both directions, with both sides needing each other in order to enrich each other. 'Partner' seeks to correct the mistakes of the colonial past, where an arrogant western Church often wrongly imposed its culture and way of life on unsuspecting peoples.

Today I work for the Methodist Church as a mission partner in a city called Chemnitz in a part of Germany that was formerly in the German Democratic Republic. During the forty years of Communist rule in the GDR, up until the fall of the Berlin wall (1989) and the reunification of Germany (1990), the Christian Church did not have it easy. Today, the legacy of the GDR regime can still be felt, as is seen by the almost 90 % of the population in this part of Germany who, not only have no interest in God or church, but who are actually convinced, self-professed atheists.

It was into this spiritual and religious context, a notably different one to my native Northern Ireland, that I came in 1998, when I heard God calling me to serve in Germany. I imagine it was in some small way similar for those other missionaries, Columbanus and his twelve companions, who set out from Bangor in the early Middle Ages. They too, left comfortable, familiar, spiritual surroundings for the unknown, entering into a world that was largely atheistic and disinterested, if not hostile.

Walking around the abbey in Bangor, I notice the bronze plaque placed near the main entrance, commemorating the missionary journey of Columbanus and the Bangor monks. The three words on the plaque—Bangor, Luxeuil, Bobbio—are the names of the three towns where Columbanus established important monasteries that became so influential in early medieval Europe. Of all three towns, I have until very recently only ever heard of Bangor, but through my preparatory reading I know that Luxeuil is in France and Bobbio is in Italy. I also know that my journey will take me to identical bronze plaques placed at the entrance to the present day abbeys in those towns.

Standing there in the drizzling rain so typical of an Ulster summer I take one last photo of the historic abbey, its patchworked sections of stone walls recounting different chapters of Bangor's history down through the centuries. The large round clock on the bell tower reminds me of the present and the journey that lies before me—the same journey that others undertook over 1400 years before me. Walking out through the fascinating old graveyard of Bangor Abbey, encompassing the remains of bygone saints and sinners, the words of the apostle Paul come to me: "Therefore, since we are surrounded by such a great cloud of witnesses, let us throw off everything that hinders and the sin that so easily entangles, and let us run with perseverance the race marked out for us." (Hebrews 12:1).

The race marked out for me will next take me to Saint Coulomb, a little coastal village in northern France, where fourteen hundred years ago, a small group of monks from Bangor drew up their skin-covered boats and first set foot on continental Europe.

Chapter 3

Us Foreigners

H aving stayed overnight with family in Carrickfergus, I gratefully accept my brother's offer to drive me into Belfast on his way to work. The half hour journey along the shore road is like a trip down memory lane for me: past Greenisland, where I went to primary school and met the girl who would later become my wife, the University of Ulster at Jordanstown where I worked as a technician in the technology department before being called to the ministry; and Whiteabbey Methodist, the church where I did my first placement as a theology student. It survived me. It's still standing.

My brother drops me off in Belfast at the Europa Bus Station—not because my destination today is Europe, as if there were other bus stations for buses taking you to the other continents. No, the bus station is commonly known as the 'Europa', due to its location beside one of Belfast's landmarks, the Europa Hotel, also known as the "most bombed hotel in Europe" (twenty-eight times during what we in Northern Ireland euphemistically call 'The Troubles'). I pay the twelve pounds sterling for a ticket to Dublin airport, where I can get a bus taking me further south to Rosslare. My plans are to take the overnight ferry from Rosslare to Cherbourg, France.

Waiting for my bus, I notice how much Belfast has changed in recent years. I left Northern Ireland for Germany in 1998, the year of the Good Friday Agreement and the beginnings of the peace process. The political progress that has occurred since then is simply staggering, and the peace dividend huge—more jobs, more investment... and more foreigners. I am pleasantly surprised to see the amount of foreigners milling around the bus station. It is the sign not only of a stable city, but also of a mature one. Maybe, at last, Belfast is growing up.

I am also aware that within a few hours I myself will again be a foreigner, and as much as I love living in Germany, my second home, it still saddens me to be leaving Northern Ireland. On the bus to Dublin I have time to reflect on what I most like about home: family and friends of course, but other things too. The sea. I miss walking around the marina at Carrickfergus Castle or a stroll along Loughshore at Jordanstown. I miss windy days—incredible, I know, but in Germany where I live I sometimes just long for a good old Norn-Iron-blow-the-cobwebs-away windy day. A turf fire—one of the delights of having lived and ministered in County Fermanagh. And I miss those other essentials of life that no Ulsterman can do without like Tescos, Cadbury's flakes and Tayto Cheese and Onion crisps.

Arriving at the bus stop in Banbridge, a teenager reminds me of something else that I love about home. As this young man is getting off the bus, he turns to the driver and says, "Thanks very much". I had forgotten that we do this in Ireland, north and south. Everyone thanks the bus driver with a "Cheers, mate" or a "Thank you, now" as they get off the bus.

This is not a done thing in Germany, not because the Germans are less grateful or polite, but simply because it's a different culture with a different way of doing things. For instance, it is customary for Germans to generally greet everyone with a *Guten Tag* when they enter the corner shop or the waiting room at the local GP's. Likewise you could be standing in the queue at the post office in Germany when someone comes in and greets all present in the room with an indirect general greeting. In Northern Ireland we would probably just come into a waiting room and quietly sit down, greeting only the people beside us. If we uttered a loud "Good Morning" on entering the room, everyone present would think we were employed there and wanted their attention for something. Similarly, we would attract strange looks in a post office if we walked in and greeted the queuing public with a loud "Good morning everyone!". We just don't do that.

We do share greetings on the street, however, which the Germans are not into. Naturally it is different on a crowded street in a town or city, but in Northern Ireland if you meet someone on a quiet street, you would normally acknowledge them with a nod and an "Alright luv?" or a "Hi ya?", even if you do not know them personally. It may even just be a comment about the weather, like, "That's a cold one", or friendly banter about what the person you are greeting happens to be doing at that very moment: "Looks like he's taking you for a walk!" (said to someone walking a large dog), or "You're making me tired just looking at you" (to a jogger), or "Hope we get the weather you're expecting!" (said to someone wearing shorts when it's cold, which it invariably is in Ireland). "Hello" works too when greeting

a stranger, but to us Ulster folk it just seems a little bit
lacking in something.

In any case, the Irish are pretty much greet-on-the-
street folk. But in Germany you can visit the doctor and
whilst sitting in the waiting room be indirectly greeted
by someone who enters the room and takes his place next
to you. You can then meet this very same person twenty
minutes later as you pass each other on an empty street
and he will walk right by you without saying a dickie bird.
No acknowledgement, no nod, no hello, *nichts*—and in
doing this he is not being ignorant or impolite. He is just
being 'foreign', doing things that are foreign or strange
to us (Northern) Irish folk, just as some of our behaviour
must seem foreign and strange to German folk.

As if God is preparing me for what is to come, and all
that will be culturally foreign to me in the coming days,
he duly arranges for me to spend the last remaining hours
of my time in Ireland with people from foreign countries.

It starts with the young backpacker from Finland I chat
to in the queue at the bus station. He has just finished
studying and is spending three months touring Europe.
Then there is the holidaying middle-aged French couple
sitting behind me on the bus whose talk is the same way
I would like my Belfast to Dublin bus service to be—non-
stop. Outside Dublin airport, I ask the rather rotund *Bus
Eireann* inspector where the bus to Rosslare leaves from.
He answers me in English, but not as I know it. I have to
concentrate hard to understand his strong Dublin brogue
directing me to bus stop number eight. There's nothing
wrong with the *Fat Controller's* whistling though, as he ably
demonstrates in gaining the attention of the Polish driver

of the bus to Rosslare who has just driven off without all of us who are waiting patiently at bus stop number eight.

We are grateful that wolf-whistle is an understood form of communication in Poland, because the Rosslare bus screeches to a halt and then starts reversing back up the road to us *wannabe* passengers. I load my rucksack into the hold and take a seat at the front of the bus, just behind the driver, who as well as appearing very stressed, also seems to be a religious man as he mutters "Jesus" and "Christ" at various times and various vehicles along the route.

Things get even more stressful for our Polish bus driver when we pull into the bus station in Dublin city centre. An inspector helps an African lady onto the bus and tells our bus driver that she wants to go to Ovoca Manor and that he should let her out at the appropriate stop. This simple request actually leads to a kind of modern day version of the biblical tale of the tower of Babel, where mankind's efforts to build a tower are thwarted by language barriers. Our Polish friend, whose English is limited, has no idea where Ovoca Manor is as it is not on the main bus route. The African lady, who has even less English, also has no idea where she is meant to get off the bus and looks increasingly worried the further we travel.

When our bus makes a routine stop in Wicklow I decide to ask a man who is boarding the bus if Ovoca Manor is anywhere nearby, but he does not understand my northern accent. I have to ask him three times before he finally understands me and is able to give me an answer. Unfortunately I don't understand what he is saying, so I ask him to repeat it, which he does again to no avail. A third time we try to build our tower and this time, unlike the biblical story, we succeed. Over the sobs of the African lady on my left and the fervent appeals to Christ spoken from Pole position on my right, I finally grasp that the Southerner is telling me that this is indeed the nearest stop to Avoca. The young lady needs to disembark here and get a different bus that will take her the remaining six miles to her destination, hopefully this time without incident.

As our coach further winds its way through some beautiful Irish countryside, interspersed with lively little coastal towns and villages, I am reminded of how confusing and frustrating language, or the lack of it, can actually be. Of course things are made even more complicated when there are different words for the same thing... like the name of our Bangor abbot.

Columbanus, Columban, Columba, Coulomb. No, not the declensions of some Latin noun, but the various names given to the leader of the group of twelve Bangor monks who set sail for France in the sixth century. It gets even more confusing because the Bangor Columba is also known as Columba the younger, which means there was a Columba the older, who also happened to be called Columcille—remember him—the missionary monk from Derry who set up shop in Iona? Add the linguistic modifications made to the name as the monks made their way through France, Germany, Austria, Switzerland and Italy, and you end up with the variations listed above, and the distinct possibility of a 'Tower of Babel' moment.

To keep things simple, I decide to stick with the name Columbanus, the Romanized form of Columba, which by the way is still popular in Ireland today in its shortened form, Colum, meaning 'dove'. Columbo, on the other hand, depending on who you talk to, is either the capital city of Sri

Lanka, or a homicide detective in a U.S. crime fiction TV series, and is not to be confused with our sixth century pilgrim.

The prayers of our Christ-invoking bus driver must have been heard because we arrive in good time at Rosslare Harbour, where *Oscar Wilde*, the ferry that will be my home for the eighteen hour journey to Cherbourg, awaits. After purchasing a ticket, one way without cabin, I make my way to the boarding gate where a large group of Italians are already waiting. I take this opportunity to find out what the Italian for 'hitchhiking' is. This could come in useful when I head to Milan and further south to Bobbio. *Autostop* does not sound very Italien, which is a bonus for me, but asking someone if you can travel with them to Milan is a little more tricky: *Vorrei un passagio per Milano?*

Boarding the ferry is relaxed and uncomplicated, a pleasant experience compared to flights on the cheap airlines I normally use where boarding can be like a frantic game of musical chairs with passengers jockeying for position so as not to be the last one standing. Perhaps someday people boarding cheap flights will notice the important difference to the real game of musical chairs—there are never fewer chairs than people playing. I have yet to see a stewardess removing a seat from the plane whilst people are boarding.

Stepping onto the ship and into the main reception area, we are greeted by a violinist and an accordion player playing soothing music belonging to the easy-listening genre. I take note that "Nearer my God to Thee" and other Titanic related tunes are absent from their repertoire. A friendly steward directs me to my recliner seat on deck ten, which is in a small compartment of twenty seats in a quieter part of the ship. There are only seven other people here and they have already staked their claims on the seats nearest to the large window with an unhindered view of the hull of a lifeboat suspended about six feet away on the deck outside. Looking around, I notice that sleeping bags have already been rolled out in the most favourable corners of the room. 'Musical chairs' has started. I join in, opening my rucksack in the aisle between two rows of seats, marking my territory and ensuring that 'when the music stops' I am not one of the losers.

My roommates for the night are bikers—apt considering Columbanus is the patron saint of motorcycles. My roommates are not Hell's Angels type bikers, but rather just ordinary folk who are touring the continent on motorcycle. There are three Estonians, a young couple from Hungary, an Italian and a Czech. I am the other 'foreigner' among them, and the only one not actually living on the island of Ireland.

I sit down and eat the two cheese and ham baps that I bought in Belfast a few hours earlier, washing it down with what's left of my coke. The bikers are engrossed in conversation, in English, their common language, but I understand very little because they are talking bikes. For the next hour and a half I am put through my very own *enduro* trial that includes hearing about givi monolock mounting hardware, E-marked headlights, the head pipe diameter of an exhaust for a CB500, and how fluffy motorcycle seats can chaff the inner thighs.

By the time I go to clear my head on the outer decks, *Oscar Wilde* is already sailing in open seas. Even though it is quite windy today, it is difficult to detect any movement at all on the ship due to the modern stabilizers she has been fitted with. Technology has obviously come a long way since the days of Columbanus who made this journey with his disciples in a *curragh*, a small open-topped sailing boat made of leather and wicker.

Personally, I am glad of the stabilizers today, even if they do give me the impression that the captain, like a small child on his bike, is still only learning and will someday be able to sail his ship without them. Standing at the rear of the ship, sheltered from the wind, I stare out over the wake that traces our progress through the Irish Sea. For a brief moment I am hypnotized by the countless whirlpools of disturbed seawater below me, twisting and turning as if dancing freestyle before falling back into formation and the greater rhythm of the sea. Deep, too.

When I arrive back to my seat, all but two of my biker roommates have gone to the bar and the compartment is quiet now with only the dull hum of the engines to be heard deep below us in the bowels of the ship. Climbing into my sleeping bag, I am glad that the floor is carpeted—although a thicker underlay would not go amiss.

We are now sailing through international waters. Here, we all are foreigners. I am reminded once again of the Polish bus driver and his courage in coming to start afresh in a foreign country where everything is new and different and difficult. I think of my biker roommates, all twentysomethings from various parts of Europe, who have come to study or work in Ireland. I understand them. I know how they feel because I myself am living and working as a foreigner in another European country. And I can't help smiling when I think of how Saint Columbanus had a hand in all this.

In 1950, Robert Schumann, one of the founding fathers of the European Community and first president of the European Parliament, described Columbanus, who achieved a spiritual union among some of the principle European countries of his time, as the patron saint of all those seeking to build a united Europe. Traveling through the chaos of Europe in the aftermath of the collapse of the Roman empire convinced Columbanus that all of Europe should be one body held together by its Christian roots, able to overcome all ethnic and cultural barriers.

If I were Columbanus, I would be waking up tomorrow morning with my boat approaching Neustria, the western part of the sixth century kingdom of the Franks. History being what it is, *Oscar Wilde* will dock in Cherbourg in present day France, where my Columban adventure will begin for real.

Although I know that it was incredibly more difficult for Columbanus when he set foot on French soil fourteen hundred years ago, it still does not stop me worrying about how things will go for me tomorrow. How will the hitchhiking work out? Will people stop for me? How far will I get? Will I be safe? Where will I sleep tomorrow night? What will tomorrow bring? Knowing my thoughts, God seeks to allay my fears. The gentle vibrations of the ship, *Oscar Wilde*, rock me to sleep, as if whispering to me the words of her namesake, another Irish ex-pat who ended up in France, "Every saint has a past and every sinner has a future."

Chapter 4

Lessons from a Talking Horse

I have slept surprisingly well on the floor despite using my shoes and a rolled-up jacket as a pillow. I think of how many different pillows I have tried out at home in the hope of finding that elusive blissful night's sleep. Now I know. When I get home, I will be putting a rain jacket and an old pair of *Converse* sneakers into a pillow case. That should do it. The ear plugs also worked a treat. I did not hear the bikers coming in from the bar last night.

After a wash and shave in the toilets on deck ten, I go down to the restaurant for breakfast—tea, orange juice, a croissant and two slices of toast. An hour later, having packed all my things together and topped up my water bottle, I am standing in the queue of foot passengers ready for disembarkment. At breakfast I had kept my eyes open for someone who possibly looked like they had space in their car—and in their hearts—for a hitchhiker. Not being able to see into their cars—nor into their hearts—my efforts proved unsuccessful.

Standing in the queue considering my options, I meet the lady I had helped as we were boarding the ship in Rosslare. She had been struggling with her luggage and I had offered to help her at the point where she could no longer use the luggage trolley. Our encounter at the boarding gate in Rosslare had been very brief and we only spoke English, but now as we disembark together, I discover that Monique is French. She also knows her way around Cherbourg and is heading into town to the main train station.

Glad to have found someone who knows where they are going and where I am meant to be going, I once again offer to help carry Monique's luggage. She accepts, deal done, and within ten minutes guide Monique and sherpa Barry are leaving the ferry terminal together to walk the two miles into the city centre.

Monique is a French teacher and has been on a sailing holiday in Ireland for the last three weeks. Her English is perfect, which makes conversation easy. I am interested to hear about her sailing escapades, and she is keen to know more about my life as a clergyman and my journey in the footsteps of Saint Columbanus. She looks surprised when I tell her that I hope to travel through France by *Autostop* (hitchhiking). She also looks surprised when I tell her that I have no idea where I will be sleeping each night. But she looks the most surprised when I tell her that my destination today is a little place in Brittany called Saint Coulomb.

"I live near Mont-Saint-Michel", she says, "It's not far from Saint Coulomb. If you don't find accommodation anywhere, you can stay at our place. No Problem." We part at Rue de la Gare, where Monique turns right to walk the remaining few yards to the train station.

"Give me a call if you get stuck", she says, writing down her phone number for me.

"I might just do that", I reply, thanking her for her kindness, *"Merci beaucoup!"*

Monique still finds it incredible that someone would come all the way from Ireland to the tiny village of St. Coulomb. *"Le petit monde!"* she says, smiling, as she throws her bag over her shoulder and turns to be on her way. "Small world indeed", I answer and then whisper to myself, "... but big God", as I acknowledge His providence. Even though I will later discover that God has other plans regarding my accommodation for tonight, I am glad that He is kind enough to let me know in advance that I have nothing to worry about today. At least I will have a roof over my head tonight. And, as so often is the case, He does it through ordinary people in everyday life; people who are not even aware that they have quite literally been an angel to someone, a modern day messenger of God.

Quite chuffed with how my first day on French soil has begun, I walk a further three kilometres along the main road with a spring in my step. I am heading for the outskirts of Cherbourg in the direction of Caen where I will begin my French hitchhiking adventure for real. According to the route planner app on my phone Saint Coulomb is only about 130 miles away, and I have all day to get there. It's a great feeling not to have any time pressures, and even though Cherbourg is not the most attractive of towns, the sun still shines on it, and on me.

After about an hour I arrive at what looks like a good spot on the road to thumb a lift. It's a long, straight stretch of uphill road with lots of lay-byes where cars can easily pull in and stop without hindering the flow of traffic. We are still within the town limits which means the cars are traveling relatively slow, increasing my chances of being picked up. I turn to face the approaching cars and stick my thumb out for a lift. The first four cars pass me by, but the fifth vehicle, a white Ford Transit van, stops.

I hurry the short distance up the hill to the waiting van and open the passenger side door. *"Bonjour Monsieur. La Direction Caen?"*

The driver, a man in his mid-twenties, babbles away to me in French of which I understand nothing, but I interpret the clearing away of papers and making space on the passenger seat as a "yes", so I throw my rucksack into the van and climb in. And so begins my very first French hitchhiking experience.

Alain, my chauffeur, can't speak English so I am forced to use my extremely rusty schoolboy French. It is painful but is actually the best thing that could happen to me as I realise that I learnt more at school than I thought. For the next hour Alain and I have a great chat even though I am still not sure we are always on the same wavelength. We talk about work and family and cars and satellite navigation and music. Then Alain puts on a CD and introduces me to the French music genre *varieté* with songs about silicon boobs and Madame Pee-Pee. Thinking it a bit much for a first date, I decide not to enquire further as to the actual content of the songs. I simply enjoy the ride, listening to traditional French music while being chauffeured through the countryside in the general direction of Saint Coulomb. Alain kindly offers to take me as far as Ducey. From there I can hitchhike up towards the coast and Saint Coulomb, my destination for today.

In Ducey I walk from the roundabout where Alain has left me to the main road leading to Saint Malo. It takes a little longer to get picked up this time, but eventually a little Romanian built *Dacia Sandero* pulls up with a mother and her teenage son in it. They are able to take me as far as Saint Malo which is not far from Saint Coulomb. I just about manage to squeeze into the back seat with my rucksack as the car is already packed full with the Dacia family's holiday luggage.

Madame Dacia is a primary school teacher. Her English is excellent and she is very talkative. This is all well and good if it were not for the fact that she is driving like a crazy woman and insists on turning round to face me every time she says something. I keep glancing up at her rear view mirror hoping she will take the hint and at least keep her head facing forwards even if her eyes are not directly on the road. But she's not taking the hint. She continues, getting quite animated when talking about her frustrations with the French schooling system and her lackadaisical pupils, and each time she speaks she turns round to face me. She is beginning to turn my head too as I watch our little Dacia drift back and forth across the white line separating us from the oncoming traffic.

I am quite sure that Saint Columbanus had to face many challenges and hazards on his travels through France in the early Middle Ages, but I am beginning to wonder if they were ever as life threatening as this. The angels are definitely on overtime for this journey, but they accomplish their mission and I am truly relieved to step out of the car on the outskirts of Saint Malo, if not in peace, at least in one piece.

The weather is ideal for walking, and since my pulse needs to come down anyway I decide to walk the remaining few miles to Saint Coulomb. There are not many cars on this road that skirts fields of crops with farmhouses scattered here and there along the route. After a while I come to a lake which looks like an ideal place for a break and something to eat. I cross the bridge, skirting round the lake until I find a suitable spot under a tree by a wooden fence and a single pile of logs.

Two horses in the field next to me watch with great interest as I proceed to set up my little methylated-spirit-fueled cooker. Pasta with chopped ham in a cream tomato sauce is the order of the day, followed by a mug of tea and the delicious *pain-au-chocolat* I bought at a *boulangerie* earlier this morning. When my horse friends realise that I am not going to share my meal with them, they quickly lose interest and go back to their diet of dandelions and daisies. I am glad they do not go too far away. I don't like dining alone.

After my meal, my tummy full, I lie back on the grass and let the sun bathe my body. Heaven. The sound of grass being munched by *Black Beauty* beside me is incredibly therapeutic. There is nothing rushed about the way the horse eats. Each bite is carefully chosen and each mouthful slowly chewed, with such rhythmic regularity that it has hypnotic effects on me.

I think of my work with all its stresses and pressures. I think of my congregation back in Germany and some of the stuff going on there: the young couple whose marriage is on the rocks; the lady who has just been diagnosed with cancer; the elderly man who is trying to come to terms with the loss of his wife; the youth group who are presently without a youth leader; the new social outreach project we are about to begin in the neighbourhood; the couple who are grieving because they can't have kids; the plans to build a new extension to the church to give us more rooms for ministry; the young man who feels called to the pastoral ministry.

I think of how little time I have—or more accurately, how little time I make—for the simple things, the important things, in life. I think of some of my colleagues or church members who have suffered burnout, and the many more who are suffering boreout. And I realise I am in danger of heading the same way too. Lying here in the sun on the banks of Étang de Sainte-Suzanne I make a mental note about my future life and ministry: take more time to listen to horses munching grass.

I can even imagine having a relaxation therapy CD made up solely of sounds of horses chewing grass. Any time I get stressed out, I can put the CD on, lie down, close my eyes and listen to the therapeutic sounds of... rip, crunch, munch... rip, crunch, munch. There could even be a market for this. If there are relaxation CDs with birdsong or whale sounds, why not for grass-munching horses too?

Just as I am imagining organizing grass-munching relaxation seminars for stressed out business managers, a tractor pulls into the field and interrupts my daydreaming. I decide that the relaxation therapy with my new horse friends will all have been for nothing if I get charged for trespassing by an irate French farmer. I quickly wash my pots and dishes in the lake, pack my things together and thank my four-legged friends for their therapy session before making my way back out onto the road.

Walking the last couple of miles to Saint Coulomb I have time to think more seriously about the importance of taking time to rest, to relax and to appreciate the simple things in life. Perhaps this was one of the strengths of the Bangor monks who made it a priority to withdraw from the busyness of everyday life at regular intervals in order to spend time in prayer, stillness and contemplation.

I can't imagine myself going as far as some Irish monks who withdrew completely from society and lived the ascetic life of a hermit. This so-called "green" martyrdom was the Irish answer to the "red" martyrdom that many Christians on the continent had suffered. "Red" martyrdom—dying violently as a martyr for your faith under persecution—was not necessary in Ireland, and so instead the Irish monks emphasized dying to self, either by means of the "green" martyrdom (the ascetic life) or the "white" martyrdom which meant leaving family and fatherland for the cause of Christ.

I am glad I do not have to face red martyrdom living as I do in a free and democratic Europe. Incredible as it seems in the twenty-first century, there are still Christians in other parts of the world who do suffer persecution and die for their faith.

I reckon that I qualify for white martyrdom. I have left family and fatherland for the cause of Christ, going overseas to serve Him in Germany. I am however a bit lacking on the green martyrdom front. I do not take enough time to be still and know that God is God. The demands and distractions of modern day life, along with my own ill-discipline, have meant that I am sometimes not as near to God as I would like to be. Nor have I always been able to hear the voice of God as clearly as I should have.

On the road to Saint Coulomb, with the sun shining warmly on my face, the wind at my back and the road rising up to meet me, I realise how easy it is to preach but how much more difficult it is to practise what I preach. It's easier to tell others what to do, than to do it yourself. I have often preached about the importance of making space for God in your life, spending time with Him and taking time out to listen to Him.

One such occasion was the Sunday I had just begun to read the scripture lesson in the church worship service when a mobile phone rang out from somewhere in the congregation. It belonged to one of the young people in our church, but instead of quickly turning his cell phone off so as not to disturb the service, he took the call. "Hello. How are you?... No, it's ok, go ahead. I'm just in church here..."

Unperturbed, I continued reading the Bible lesson to the congregation. I was beginning to sense I did not have their full attention when a second mobile phone began to ring. A young man near the back of the church answered his phone and he too began a conversation with the caller. "Hi. Good to hear from you... Hold on a minute. I don't have great reception here." He got up from his pew and made his way to the nearest window. "That's better. What can I do for you?..."

I continued reading God's word from the front of the church as all this commotion was going on in the background. Then, unbelievably, a third mobile phone rang. And, even more unbelievably, it was not immediately turned off but answered and a conversation begun. By this stage many church members were looking around incredulously, obviously irritated that people could be so inconsiderate and disrespectful.

The three telephone calls ended just as I was finishing reading the Bible lesson. I closed the Bible, placing it back on the altar and then turned to face the congregation.

"Tell me, brothers and sisters, were you able to hear God's word today?"

Some church members were indignant. "No. We couldn't hear a thing. There were too many distractions. It's a disgrace!"

As I looked around the congregation I could see some people knowingly smiling. They knew what I was up to. The remainder of the congregation then also smiled, some shaking their head, as I proceeded to explain that I had arranged the whole thing with the young people beforehand. I had asked three members of my youth group to carry out mock conversations on their mobile phones during the reading of the Scriptures in church that morning.

Looking my flock in the eye, I drove the important point home that I was hoping to teach them: "Is that not how it often is in everyday life? God speaks to us, he communicates with us, he shares things with us and seeks to guide and direct us. He longs to be a part of our life. But we simply do not hear his voice because there are so many other voices demanding our attention, so many other distractions. Why not take time to listen to the One who wants to bless us more than we know."

Reflecting on all this as I approach the outskirts of Saint Coulomb, I realise again how important it is to go back to basics on a regular basis. On too many occasions in recent months I have let other voices drown out the still small voice of God. Too often I have let urgent things take

44

priority over important things. Too often I have majored on doing things right instead of doing the right things. Today, lying in the sun by the banks of a small lake in northern France God uses a horse to remind me of this. It's just one of his gifts to me this day.

Not wanting to look a gift horse in the mouth, I smile and gratefully accept the gentle nudging of God's Spirit on my life.

Chapter 5

Any Friend of Columbanus is a
Friend of Mine

I arrive in the little village of Saint Coulomb around tea time. There is not much to it really, the main focal point being L'eglise Saint-Columban, the church that bears the name of the monk the village is named after. I buy *une bouteille d'eau* in the little shop on the corner and sit down on the steps of the church to drink it.

I have made good progress today, arriving at my intended destination in good time to look around and find a bed for my first night on the continent. I am realising however that it could be difficult finding accommodation here. The place is so small. I comfort myself with the thought that I can always make my way back to Monique and her family if things don't work out for me here.

But I still have one ace up my sleeve. When I was researching and preparing for this trip I got some help from a retired Councillor on Bangor City Council. Marsden Fitzsimons was kind enough to give me a couple of names and addresses of people on the continent who could possibly be of help to me.

Sitting on the steps of *l'eglise de Saint-Columban* I open up my notebook and check Marsden's list. I am in luck.

Monsieur Marcel Moreau lives here. He is a member of *Les Amis Bretons de Columban* (Friends of Clumbanus, Brittany), a group that celebrates the life and ministry of the Irish saint, Columbanus. Through an app on my phone I discover that the street where Monsieur Moreau lives is only round the corner. Small villages do have their plus points.

Five minutes later I am standing ringing the doorbell, unannounced, of a complete stranger in Sleepyville, France. Needless to say, I am nervous. The door opens and a fit-looking sixty-something year old man wearing grey trousers, a white shirt, and blue pullover is standing before me. His brown sandals and white socks complete the continental look. I smile. A smile is universal. It builds bridges. I am hoping it does so here.

"Bonjour Monsieur. Je m'appelle Barry Sloan. Je viens de Bangor, Irlande du Nord. Je..."

As soon as Monsieur Moreau hears the word "Bangor", a smile comes to his face. He interrupts my stuttering French and invites me warmly into his home. He calls his wife, introducing me to her, as he takes my rucksack from me. *"Enchanté, Madame Moreau"*, I say, delighted that my French, although poor, has not deserted me altogether. Over the course of the next three days my language skills will improve considerably simply because my hosts do not speak English at all.

Within ten minutes of meeting them, not only have Monsieur and Madame Moreau told me that I am to stay for dinner, but have also offered me accommodation in the spare bedroom in their home. I gladly accept, relieved and delighted at how God is watching out for me.

Madame Moreau has prepared a fine three-course meal with wine and cheese to round it off. I could get used to this—*c'est la vie* of a Frenchman! The Moreaus are a special couple—pious, very involved in their local church. Victor is also one of the leading lights in the local Saint Coulomb branch of "The Friends of Saint Columbanus". I had never heard of this organization before and was interested to learn that it aims to promote the pioneer missionary spirit of Columbanus and the other Bangor monks who set out in the early Middle Ages to spread the gospel of God's love throughout Europe. The "Friends", are mainly from a Roman Catholic background and have branches in many parts of Europe and North America. On my travels through France, Austria, Switzerland and Italy I will discover that some of them, like the Moreau family, will also become friends to me.

It has been a long day and I am tired. Communicating in French, having to listen so intently and constantly searching to find the right words has been exhausting. Thanking my hosts again for their hospitality I say my goodnights, briefly petting their cute little dog, "Poopsie" (I did not ask about the name—I think I can imagine), before having a quick shower and falling into bed.

The plain little bedroom is made homely by the oil paintings painted by Madame Moreau herself. A large antique oak wardrobe stands at the end of my double bed and dominates the room. On the wall to the right of me, above the door, hangs a plain wooden cross. An excellent painting of a semi-nude woman is hanging on the wall to the left of me.

I set the digital alarm clock on my bedside table to waken me at seven, and then lie in bed meditating and reflecting on my day. It has been a blessed day, perfect in many ways, except one. My wife, Gill, is not here with me.

Ignoring the naked woman to my left, I turn to face the cross, before closing my eyes and drifting off to sleep.

Breakfast is at eight, typically continental with baguette, confiture and *jus d'orange*. Tea being served in a large cereal bowl with a table spoon may well be continental but it is not typical for me. I decide to take my time drinking a glass of orange juice in order to watch how my hosts tackle their tea. I learn that the French custom is to dip your baguette into the tea, or to use your spoon as you would with soup. (Either that, or the Moreaus are still laughing about the trick with the 'bowl of tea' that they played on that Irish guy). Whatever. I follow suit, and tablespoon my tea into me. Lovely jubbly.

Marcel has offered to show me the beach where Saint Columbanus and his twelve companions landed, all those centuries ago. We drive out towards the coast, the country roads narrowing as we climb our way up to a vantage point on the cliffs overlooking the sea. We park the car and walk the last few hundred yards to the top. Our efforts have not been in vain. Scattered below us in both directions along the rocky coastline are the most beautiful sandy beaches, repeatedly kissed by wave after wave of atlantic tide. Looking down over the splendour of this stretch of Bretagne coastline it is easy to understand why the Bangor monks would choose to pull their boats up on shore at this spot. What I don't understand is why they ever left here.

The weather is good today and there are already some people bathing—in the sea and in the sun. On the roadside nearby is a large stone cross erected to mark the landing of those early Irish Christians who were to change the face of Europe. I wonder if the sunbathers are aware of the stone cross they have walked past in order to get onto the beach. Do they know its meaning, its purpose? Or are they like the individuals who stood around another cross two thousand years ago—the one at Calvary on which Jesus was crucified—present, but completely oblivious to its significance? As I ponder this, I am reminded that God didn't give up on those folk two thousand years ago when they failed to recognize his plan for their lives. For the sunbathers on a beach in present day France He hasn't changed.

The people of the town of Saint Coulomb are known locally as *les Columbanais,* and over the next couple of days, I get to meet some of them, along with a few of the "Brittany Friends of Saint Columba". The Friends give me a guided tour of the church with its exquisite marble statues and poignant stained glass windows of Saint Paul and Saint Columbanus, two pioneers whose own missionary journeys transformed continents. When I ask what is in the glass case at the foot of Saint Columbanus' statue, I am told it is a relic of the good man himself—a small piece of one of Columbanus' bones.

In the Middle Ages, tales of the healing properties of the remains (relics) of the saints became popular, and soon every altar was expected to exhibit one. Even though I have read stories in the Bible about the Prophet Elisha's bones healing a dead man or the apostle Paul's handkerchief being imbued with healing powers, this relic thing is totally alien to me. It is however common practice in the Catholic church, as I will discover on my journey through Europe. Considering the fact that the remains of Saint Columbanus are buried in the church in Bobbio, Italy, I am amazed at how many other churches and chapels claim to have relics of him. I guess it is a good thing that Columbanus was over six foot tall.

In Protestant churches the pulpit is often the main focal point in the church, expressing the importance of the preaching of the word of God. But here in l'eglise de Saint Coulomb, as in most Catholic churches, the altar takes central place, underlining the importance of Jesus' sacrifice when the congregation celebrates the Eucharist, Holy Communion. The distinguishing feature on this altar is the fascinating wooden relief carving of the landing of the monks from Bangor.

I am glad to meet the local man responsible for the handmade banner of Saint Columbanus hanging in the church. The banner depicts Columbanus at sea in a small boat with the French coastline in the background, above him the word "Bangor", and below him the words "Saint Coulomb". *Les Amis* are obviously proud of their Bangor connection. So much so, in fact, that their association helped organize a trip to Northern Ireland in 2010, visiting Bangor Abbey and bringing greetings to their Christian brothers and sisters there.

On a tour of the village of Saint Coulomb I try to imagine what this place was like back in the sixth century when the Bangor missionaries first arrived. Were they well received? Christianity had been able to take root in most of the towns throughout the Roman empire, but the countryside was still largely pagan. All this was soon to change, largely through the influence of missionary monks such as Columbanus and those who went out from the monasteries he would later establish, but I wonder how the Irish monks were treated when they landed here. Were the natives friendly? Was the hospitality as good as that which I have been enjoying? What challenges and difficulties did the Irish monks face?

Whatever the challenges were, it seems they were all overcome, as Columbanus and the Bangor monks were able to have a significantly positive impact on this region. Otherwise the little town of Saint Coulomb, if it existed at all today, would surely only do so under a different name. I think of the message the Bangor monks brought with them, the gospel of God's love, demonstrated in Jesus Christ, and how this message was communicated not only in words, but also in practical ways that made a real difference to people's lives. And I think about the work of the present day church in Saint Coulomb as it endeavours to share that same gospel message of God's love for a broken world.

I am reminded of the brokenness of this world as I sit alone in the church in St. Coulomb. On the pew beside me is a handwritten note, left there intentionally by someone. I admire the beautiful script—a lady's handwriting, neat, tidy, the French words written in perfectly straight lines and easily legible even though written on un-ruled paper. Immaculately conceived. As I begin to read, I realise it is a prayer to a saint, *la prière à Saint Rita*. I didn't even know there was a Saint Rita, and even if I did I would never think of praying to her. It's just not part of my tradition to pray to the saints. In my tradition we pray to Jesus, who acts as mediator and intercessor for us before God. Like I said before, we Protestants don't really do saints.

But this prayer touches me. I am moved by the profound simplicity of the words and the intense yearning of the one praying them. Even though the name Rita doesn't sound very spiritual to me, the fact that this prayer should be directed to her is also significant. Saint Rita is known in the Roman Catholic church as the saint of lost causes. She was born in Italy in the fourteenth century and was abused by her husband for many years. After his death, she became a nun and dedicated her life to God. Abused women pray to Saint Rita, asking her to intercede for them in their impossible causes. I read the prayer again, this time translating as I read.

Precious, powerful Saint Rita, advocate of desperate causes. Hear my prayer.

Ease my pain. Alleviate my distress. Take away my sorrows.

Saint Rita, protect me. Saint Rita, guard me. Saint Rita, answer me.

Two thoughts are going through my mind as I sit in the silence of the empty church. Firstly, my heavenly Father heard that prayer, even if it was not directly addressed to Him. He is big enough to not have to need the intercessory prayers of saints, but He is also big enough to allow or indeed welcome the intercession of the saints. My God is the God of desperate cases and lost causes. He hears those kinds of prayers, no matter who they come from, or through.

The other thought that is going through my mind has to do with the text that is attached to the bottom of the prayer. As much as I am moved by the desperate plight of the needy person praying, I am equally disturbed by this text, which to me is nothing less than an abuse of the prayer. I read that whoever finds this written prayer will receive an extraordinary blessing from God if they copy it fifteen times and distribute the copies each time they come to church.

People who are suffering and in desperate need are often most susceptible to this kind of thinking which links prayer to performance, in the sense of: If you just do enough, or appease God enough, He will bless you. Such thinking may well have been en vogue in Saint Columbanus' day in the Middle Ages, but I personally find it today not only obnoxious, but indeed dangerous. I believe in a loving, gracious God. Not in one who waits until I have done Him enough favours before He helps me.

On my final day in Saint Coulomb Marcel takes me to meet another man of the cloth—no, not the local window cleaner—the local priest. Père Jean Michel Roginski, an unassuming man with a keen intellect, came into the priesthood later in life. I am sure that this is one of the reasons why he connects so easily with the ordinary man on the street. It is interesting to hear of the difficulties and challenges facing the church in rural northern France, and to recognize how they are in many ways similar to my east German context, different as it is: church membership is declining, young people are moving away to the cities to study or find work, and parishes are being asked to amalgamate, with pastors having charge of increasing numbers of churches.

I am glad of the time that Père Roginski takes from his busy schedule for me, to answer my questions, and share his vision for the future. Here is a man from a different country to mine, a different church to mine, and in many ways a different theological understanding of the Christian faith to mine. And yet, a man who by God's grace is doing his bit to make the world a better place, one life at a time. I thank Father

Roginski for his genuinely warm welcome. I share with him that it is Saint Columbanus who has brought me, a Northern Irish Protestant, to this Roman Catholic church today. And I tell him that Northern Ireland still needs that same life-changing, reconciling gospel that Columbanus preached all those years ago. We both stand at the front of the church, at the foot of the cross that, despite our differences, unites us, and pray the Lord's Prayer together—he in French, me in English. Different, but the same.

Chapter 6

Le Mans 24h

Marcel has kindly offered to drive me to Chateauneuf, a main intersection where I will have a better chance of getting a lift to Rennes. Driving through Cancale I get a glimpse over the bay to Le Mont-St-Michel, a picturesque tidal island dominated by its historic abbey church. In Chateauneuf I say my goodbyes to Marcel, thanking him and his wife for their kindness and generosity. I promise to send him and Madame Moreau a postcard from Bobbio in Italy should I ever get that far.

There is already one guy standing at the roadside hitchhiking so I walk further up the hill to find my own space to try my luck. Using a black marker pen I write 'Rennes' in large capital letters on a sheet of A4 paper and hold it out for the passing motorists to see. 'Rennes' is a town in northwest France, but inwardly I am hoping it is also French for, "Please take pity on this hitchhiker".

I am heading for Rennes because it is on the direct route to Luxeuil-les Bains, where Columbanus spent twenty years and founded three monasteries. After about ten minutes standing at the roadside with my makeshift sign, a classy Mercedes 4x4 Off-Roader pulls up. Carefully setting my rucksack onto the non-imitation leather seats, I climb into the back, chuffed with myself that I will be traveling in style today.

My chauffeur Jean and his wife Suzanne are from Paris and are on their way to the coast for their summer holidays. Jean is an architect (I guess that explains the car) and Suzanne works for French television... wait for it... on a religious affairs programme called *Présence Protestante*. There are so few Protestants in France that it is incredible to me that I 'just happen' to be on the road today with one of them who works full time in religious affairs for French TV. It gets even more spooky when I hear that Jean had already driven past me once but then turned his car around and came back to pick me up because his wife suggested it. *Quelle surprise!* Or maybe God just has a sense of humour.

"We wouldn't pick just anybody up", Suzanne says, breaking the ice, "but you look sensible." That's a relief. I was worried that my grey hair would be a disadvantage for me when hitchhiking. Instead of looking like a forty-five year old working his way through some kind of midlife crisis by hiking through Europe, I look 'sensible'. I'll settle for that.

Jean and Suzanne are a lovely couple and I enjoy their company. I even get to meet their son, well not actually in the flesh, just over the phone. Their teenage son who is staying with his granny for a few days has just called with some bad news. I get to hear the whole conversation because the car phone is on hands-free. Someone has died, but my poor French means I can't make out who. As so often is the case in all areas of life, hearing and understanding are not necessarily the same thing.

I can see that Suzanne is moved by what she is hearing. Jean and Suzanne exchange one of those brief glances that say a thousand words. This is not looking good. I am thinking the granny has died and here I am, a complete stranger, right in the middle of such a private moment when the news is broken to the family. I know it is good to have a clergyman present on such occasions, but is this for real?

Maybe I was meant to be in this car today for this very purpose, to be there for this particular family in their hour of need when they hear the sad news of granny's passing away? Spooky, I know, but these are the thoughts that are going through my mind as I watch and listen to Suzanne on the phone, trying to console her son who is obviously upset.

I am preparing myself for the worst when Suzanne turns to me and asks me in English if I would like to speak to the granny. It turns out a kitten that the boy had found yesterday had died during the night—upsetting, but not the end of the world—and now the granny, who lived in the US for a few years, is keen to practise her English with me. Having in my mind already just mourned granny's sudden passing away, I am relieved to hear her voice—strong, healthy, vibrant, indeed very much as I would expect from someone who has just been raised from the dead.

Jean and Suzanne, who are heading further south, are kind enough to go out of their way, driving around the ring road to leave me off east of Rennes at a tiny place called Noyal-sur-Vilaine. From here I should have a straight run to Le Mans, home of motorsport's twenty-four hour race. As it happens, I will have my own test of endurance and stamina in trying to get away from Noyal-sur-Vilaine, which by the way just happens to be an anagram of 'aerily nonvisual'. Enough said.

I am at a busy roundabout just off the main motorway between Rennes and Le Mans. As well as the roads leading to the motorway, there are some minor roads coming off the roundabout leading to other local no-name places of little importance. There is also a huge logistics and distribution warehouse right beside the roundabout, which means that almost every tenth vehicle that passes is a freight truck.

I notice a young couple standing hitchhiking, also heading for Le Mans. I ask them how long they have been here and am surprised when they tell me they have been trying to get a lift for over an hour. But it doesn't really worry me. After all, I do look sensible, and I myself have never had to wait longer than thirty minutes to get picked up. I move round to the other side of the roundabout, feeling confident in myself and present my new handmade sign "Le Mans" to the approaching motorists.

Two hours and six hundred and seventy-three cars later I am still standing at this God-forsaken roundabout with a sign for 'Le Mans', but no sign of being picked up. My fellow hitchhikers have either been successful or have actually started walking the motorway to Le Mans, which would not surprise me. In any case, I am now able to move up to their spot which is definitely better to where I had been standing. It is twenty-seven degrees Celsius and the sun is ruthlessly beating down on me, my T-shirt already damp with sweat. After a few more minutes of car counting, I begin to wilt in the heat. I have been drinking water, but I need to ration my supplies to have enough to cook a meal.

Speaking of meals... I walk down one of the minor roads off the roundabout and find a quiet spot in the shade. Glad to be out of the sun, I take a few minutes to rest, before

starting to prepare my main meal for the day. The hassle of
not getting picked up disappears as I tuck into my pasta with
cream sauce and the two delicious *Baguettes au Chambon*
Madame Moreau had packed for me early this morning.
Washing it all down with a good mug of tea, I am ready to
continue the Le Mans 24h race again.

This time I have a different tactic. I reckon I may have
a better chance of getting a lift by using a bit of humour,
something that might endear me to a passing motorist. I
decide to combine this with what I call the Ireland factor.
If folk know I am from Ireland, I believe this may be in
my interest. After all, everyone loves the Irish (I hope!).
I take out my black marker and write, *"D'Irlande à..."*,
and then I draw a cute little picture of the Eiffel tower
with a smiley beside it. I am hoping people will decipher
my message—that I have come from Ireland and am
traveling through Le Mans on my way to see the Eiffel
Tower in Paris. The fact that I do not actually want to go
Paris is irrelevant. As long as I get as far as Le Mans I
will be happy. Desperate I know, but desperate times call
for desperate measures. The thought of sleeping rough
tonight in the middle of this roundabout is not particularly
appealing to me.

The reactions from the motorists to my new sign are
encouraging. Many of them smile, or wave, some shaking
their heads and laughing. But, and it is a significant 'but',
they do not stop. Car after car drives past presenting me
with plenty of time to undertake a brief psychological
analysis of the drivers and their passengers as they whizz by.

Some people for instance purposely look the other way,
giving the impression that they haven't seen me, when in

fact we both know they have. Others suddenly have the impulse to be busy adjusting their car radio just at that very moment as they pass me by. I guess I must just happen to be standing in a little pocket of really poor radio reception. Then there are those who look at you with an apologetic smile and a gallic shrug of the shoulders, as if to say they would love to pick me up if the car wasn't already full, when in reality they are probably glad to have the excuse that their car is full as they drive past.

There are also the disinterested truckers who have already been there, done that and got the T-shirt. Or the nosey parkers, who take their eyes off the road and stare so much they nearly cause an accident. And the zombies who drive past with lifeless, expressionless faces and a heart of stone, trapped in their own sad worlds.

Alright, maybe I have been standing in the sun too long. I am obviously just trying to deal with my own rejection by projecting my frustrations onto others, in this case innocent French motorists who are under no obligation to stop for some stranger standing at a motorway roundabout. Nevertheless, the ones I find most fascinating are the cars where you can see that the wife is prepared to stop, but the husband who is driving, is not. This confirms to me my belief that the world would be a much better place if women were in the driving seat!

The exit from the roundabout where I have been standing actually leads both to Rennes and to Le Mans, which are in entirely different directions. Looking further round the corner, I notice that all the cars exiting the roundabout here take the road to Rennes. Even though the exit I am standing at also serves Le Mans, no cars head in this direction when they pass me. I stand here for another hour and watch all the cars taking the Rennes-Le Mans exit actually only head for Rennes. Why does no one take the slip road to Le Mans?! Does anyone at all live in Le Mans, or is it just open during the 24 hour race? I am totally baffled.

After another half hour baking in the sun without even the sniff of a car heading in the direction of Le Mans, let alone taking me with them, I have no other choice but to change my plans and head into Rennes. Perhaps from Rennes I will have more luck getting to Le Mans and as a last resort, I can always travel by train if I have to.

I take out my Rennes sign again and hold it out to the passing motorists. Finally a little Peugeot van stops and I am on my way. Goodbye Noyal-sur-Vilaine, and good riddance! In no time I am at the outskirts of Rennes at a major junction of the main road leading to Le Mans. I thank my little Peugeot knight in shining armour for rescuing me from the villainous roundabout of despair and enabling this pilgrim to progress, even if it is strictly speaking in the wrong direction. I try to console myself by being philosophical about it—sometimes a step backwards is the necessary thing to do in order to go forwards. I call it the theology of the cha-cha-cha.

The heat is almost unbearable and I am glad that the spot where I am standing is in the shade under a motorway flyover. I set my rucksack down on the path beside me and hold out my sign for Le Mans, the town where apparently no one lives and no one visits. An hour later I am still standing at the same spot and beginning to feel the need for a CD with the therapeutic sounds of horses munching grass in a field.

It has been a frustrating day's hitchhiking and my morale is low. It is getting late. Admitting defeat, I decide to call it a day and head for the train station. I walk into the city centre and buy a ticket to Le Mans, the town where nobody lives. Within an hour I am sitting comfortably in the train, glad to be making progress, but still a little concerned that the train is almost empty. I am beginning to think that I will be disembarking at a ghost town, like something out of an Alfred Hitchcock movie.

I arrive in Le Mans at shortly after nine o'clock, and on exiting the *Gare du Mans* I am relieved to find signs of life. The streets are bustling with night life, the cafes and bars are packed. These folk have probably been sitting here in these cafes all day long. I consider this to be totally inconsiderate of them. Maybe if they had bothered to make an excursion to Rennes today, I would have had more success at hitchhiking.

I had hoped to find a couch for the night over the internet, but I can't get the couch-surfing app on my not-so-smart-phone to load the site properly, which means I now need to find a room for the night somewhere. Even though I have not had much success today, I am not overly concerned. An iPhone app shows me the hotels and guest houses nearby and I head for the cheapest. The lady on the reception is very friendly and helpful. I like her even more when she agrees to give me bed and breakfast for 30. Le Mans is not so bad after all.

I take a hot shower to ease some of the aches in my shoulders. My packed rucksack weighs twelve kilos, probably two or three kilos too much for my trip, and I obviously was not wearing it properly today. I should have been carrying more of the weight on my hips rather than on my shoulders, but I just got lazy and careless today while I was standing at the roadside for long periods without buckling up my rucksack properly. I will know better tomorrow.

I spend some time looking at the map to determine my route for tomorrow. I can't afford to have another day like today. I basically have two options: one involves more motorway heading up and across through Troyes, with the chance of being stranded at an isolated motorway junction, like earlier today in Noyal-sur-Vilaines. The other is a more direct route heading east on mainly minor roads, with the danger of less traffic and slower progress. Both of these options will take me through Orléans. What I don't know at this stage is that God has a third option in mind for me, which will bypass Orléans altogether.

Lying in bed I talk to God about my day, the ups and the downs. We talk about how fickle I can be, how quick I am to lose heart. And how today I lost my focus and forgot to realise there is a joy in the journey, even when the journey does not go as planned, or when waiting is a part of the journey. I told God that I found it difficult to understand why Saint Columbanus would want to put himself through such a journey, a hundred times more difficult than what I experienced today. Knowing our Irish weather, I can understand why those monks left Bangor, but why did they ever leave the paradise of Bretagne with its beautiful coastline, sunny beaches, picturesque villages and hospitable people?

God listens quietly to my questioning and lets me vent my frustration. Then He answers. He doesn't always—or at least I don't always hear His answer. But this time He does. He reminds me that Columbanus and his brothers were missionaries, quite literally 'sent ones'. They were following His call on their lives, a call not to a life of comfort and personal gain, but rather to a life of service, a life of sacrifice, ironically and paradoxically to a life of complete fulfillment. I know this is a difficult concept to grasp. It is so counter-cultural, going against all that we are bombarded with in today's media, with its constant message, "You want to be happy? Look after number one!" But this is not the logic of the gospel. God's ways are not our ways. His thoughts are higher than our thoughts.

In the stillness of my hotel bedroom, God gently reminds me of my own calling—to serve, to follow, to sacrifice. I talk to Him about the new position in the German Methodist church that I have been asked to take on. He listens to me as I explain how easy it would be for me to stay in my present position as pastor in Chemnitz, the city I have grown to love. Then he reminds me that I too am a 'sent one', on the move, called to go where He sends, even if that means leaving my comfort zone and embarking on a journey into the unknown.

The journey will continue tomorrow, heading east in the direction of Luxeuil, with Orléans as my first port of call. At least that is the plan, but I should know better. The best way to make God laugh is to make plans.

Chapter 7

Breakfast with Vikings, and Other Near-Death Experiences.

I get up at 7 am and go downstairs for breakfast. I am alone in the dining room, ideal for me, as I am not a morning person. Sitting in silence, I enjoy my cereal, orange juice, a pot of tea and the best croissant I have ever tasted in my entire life. Just as I am finishing drinking my tea, a middle-aged Danish couple comes into the dining room. I know they are Danes because they are wearing Denmark T-shirts emblazoned with a large Viking ship motif.

I find it quite ironic that I am sitting here having breakfast with folk whose ancestors plundered and pillaged their way through my country in the late eighth and early ninth centuries. In fact, on my way to Bobbio in Italy I will pass through Milan, where the Bangor Antiphonary (Psalm book) is kept, intentionally carried there to safety by medieval monks fleeing the aforementioned Viking invaders.

Bangor was plundered in the year 823 and again the following year, this time killing bishop, clergy, doctors and scholars before moving on to nearby Movilla Abbey to wreak havoc there. The Annals of Ulster record how the Norsemen moved from the coastal monasteries inland up the rivers, sometimes even carrying their longships overland to set up raiding fleets on Lough Erne or Lough Neagh. They plundered Armagh three times in one month in the year 832, and in 837 all the churches of Lough Erne including Clones and Devenish, were destroyed by the pagans.

Ireland was easy prey for the Viking invaders because she was split into so many warring kingdoms, making united opposition impossible. Now why does that not surprise me? Ulster bore the brunt of the initial raids and suffered much at the hands of the Vikings, but the Ulster kings did have some successes in repelling the barbarian invaders. Eventually, the formidable resistance of Ulster led the invaders to concentrate their attacks further south.

Sitting in the dining room watching with disdain how my Danish neighbour ruthlessly devours his cornflakes, it's not hard for me to imagine how his marauding Viking ancestors crushed and crunched their way through my homeland. I decide it is time to leave before I say something that gets me into trouble.

After checking out, I make my way through deserted streets towards the outskirts of the city. Le Mans is eerily quiet. Where is everyone? Are they already sitting in the cafes? Or maybe today is the day they all go to Rennes? I wonder if it will be as difficult getting out of this place as it was to come here.

It takes me about ninety minutes to walk to the ring road around Le Mans with the main junction leading to Orléans, and even though there is a light drizzle of rain to cool me, I am sweating. I change my wet T-shirt at the roadside and hold out my new cardboard sign, marked 'Orléans', to the oncoming motorists. After fifteen minutes I decide to do away with the sign, in an attempt to get further along this road, at least as far as the next major roundabout that connects to the motorway for Chartres and Paris.

My plan works. I am picked up within five minutes by a man heading to Chartres. He drops me off at the motorway roundabout and I walk about a mile further east to a decent and safe spot for hitchhiking. After about a half an hour I get a lift with a young man called Francois, who has a Jamaican father and a French mother. He takes me as far as Bouloire, a pleasant little village on the D357. I decide not to have lunch here, but rather to press on. A father and son, on their way back home from a trade fair, are able to take me another few miles along the road. I am now about ten miles from a small town named St. Calais.

Progress has been slow so far today, which forces me to review my hitchhiking techniques. I have realised that hitchhiking is like fly-fishing. As well as a healthy dose of patience, the secret of fly-fishing is the presentation—how you present the right bait in the right place at the right time. The same is true of hitchhiking. The bait has to look attractive to the 'fish' passing by in their cars. I have discovered that jeans and a T-shirt work fine for me. When I wear my sunglasses and baseball cap, the fish are not interested.

The presentation is important: I turn to face the fish as they approach me. Simply holding out your thumb while walking with your back to them, is unlikely to get a bite. The fish need to see the bait clearly. I find that a smile usually helps, but not too forced, not too cheesy—no fish is going to take a fly if it knows it is artificial.

It is also very important to let your rucksack be seen by the fish, or even better, a rucksack and a map. This increases your chances of being spotted by the fish and makes you more interesting to them. Let's face it, what fish is going to stop for some grey-haired guy standing casually at the side of the road? He could be some loser just waiting to take advantage of your kindness. But give this guy a rucksack and a street map, and he suddenly becomes an interesting travel-the-world dude who is bound to have loads of interesting stories to tell. I always have my rucksack and a map in view when hitchhiking, but I'm still working on the travel-the-world-dude-with-interesting-stories bit.

I am on an isolated stretch of road in the middle of nowhere about ten miles west of St. Calais, and as there is no safe place to hitchhike from, I decide to walk. The vast majority of traffic is made up of lorries and motor homes There are no footpaths, which means I am continually stepping off the road onto the grass verge to allow these large vehicles to pass by. My worries are compounded by the undulating nature of the road, making the hundred yards beyond the brow of the hills particularly treacherous, as I am out of the line of sight of the approaching motorists until the very last minute.

As I cautiously make my way along truckers' alley, I am not surprised by the number of dead animals I find at the roadside: six rabbits (or hares—for me it's hard to tell even when they are not in 2D-format); four rats, three hedgehogs, something resembling a flattened baby elephant, and one bat, who either had a dodgy radar system, or the French military have developed some kind of stealth truck and use this road as a nighttime test stretch.

I need to get off this road as quickly as possible, but I am not having much luck with fly-fishing today. Some days are just like that—the fish are not taking the bait and it's frustrating. Keeping close into the side of road, I walk briskly to cover as much ground as quickly as possible. Every now and again I stop, presenting the bait to the approaching fish. Without success.

Apart from a few houses here and there, there is nothing much else on this stretch of road. I am therefore all the more surprised when I come across a huge stone cross erected in a field at the side of the road. It is not uncommon to find a stone cross, crucifix or small shrine of the Virgin Mary erected at junctions and crossroads in France and other parts of Catholic Europe. But this cross, adorned with a disproportionally small figure of the crucified Christ, seems totally out of place here on this long straight in the middle of nowhere.

I set down my rucksack to take a picture as cars drive past, their occupants more interested in me than in the focus of my attention. In my teens I was expected to treat the crucifix with disgust. It was a symbol of Roman Catholicism. 'Our' cross, the Protestant cross, didn't have Jesus hanging on it.

Even though we rarely saw the inside of a church, and had no real interest in the Christian faith, in our narrow-minded, black and white world of Protestant bigotry, the cross was 'good', the crucifix 'bad'. As anyone who has grown up in Northern Ireland will know, emblems and symbols, especially religious ones, are often seen by the other side of the sectarian divide as a provocation, a threat. It is incredible how much venom the sight of a crucifix can cause in the dark hearts of some misguided people. When I myself came to faith in my late teens and started wearing a small cross on my jacket, I was asked by one of my friends why I was wearing "that fenian thing". It saddens me to think how Christ's death on the cross, a demonstration of God's love for humanity, can become for some people the very opposite—a divisive symbol of sectarian hatred and religious bigotry.

Today, standing at the side of the road looking up at this statue of the crucified Christ hanging on a stone cross, I feel no disgust, no resentment, no hatred. Nor do I on the other hand wish to worship this statue, or touch it in a superstitious way in order to receive a blessing, as is the practice of many Catholic pilgrims who visit religious shrines. No, to me this is just a statue. But it is also a symbol, a pointer, a reminder. It points to and reminds me of nothing less than my saviour and His infinite love for me.

This reminder, this message of encouragement, comes to me at just the right moment. I have been quite frustrated today. Yes, I have been picked up and taken a few miles by a few cars, but there have been hundreds of other cars that have simply ignored me and driven past. I know I have alternatives. I can always get a bus or a train or even a taxi if need be. I also have the safety net of a credit card and know that I can book into a hotel, if I have to. And yes, I am actually on a sort of holiday. It's an adventure. I don't have a deadline, I don't really have to be somewhere by a certain time. So I should actually be more relaxed about it all.

But what if I had no alternatives? No credit cards? No guarantees of a bed for the night? No money? It is frustrating enough for me to watch the cars drive past without stopping. It gets quite demoralising watching car after car after car drive past you as though you do not even exist.

"Don't you know I am a pastor?", I want to scream at them. "I have a wife and two kids. I am not some maniac. People actually like me!"

But as you stand there at the side of the road with your cardboard sign, your rucksack and your roadmap, you have no claims, no honours. Who you are and what you've done counts for nothing, because the people driving past have obviously no idea who you are or what you've done. They don't know and they don't care how important, how good, or what a great person you may or may not be.

All of this matters not one bit. You are simply depending on the kindness of someone's heart to take pity on you and not drive by without offering to help. They do not have to help. You certainly have not earned their help. You are literally depending on their unmerited favour—the Bible calls it grace. It really is that simple. You are depending on someone helping you, someone sharing their possessions with you, someone not ignoring you and not passing by on the other side of the road.

In normal life most people usually have everything under control. Most people are self reliant and independent. They manage things, plan things, decide things and accomplish things. They function. And usually without a second thought and without needing help from others. But standing as a hitchhiker at the side of the road in a foreign country you become aware of your basic dependence on others. You do not have the say anymore; you need others. You suddenly become aware of your limitations. Your doubts and insecurities set in: why are they not stopping for me? Do I look dodgy or suspect? Is it what I am wearing? Am I a mess? Am I a sad case? Is it my bags? Do I have too much baggage for people to carry? Don't people trust me? Don't they like me?

Standing at the foot of a stone cross on a busy carriageway with heavy goods vehicles speeding past, I see an image of perfect grace—Christ whose unmerited love knows no boundaries. I look up at the figure of Christ hanging on this cross, and am reminded of the One who again and again stops to help. Yes, even though He sees me as I am—on numerous occasions a mess, frequently dodgy or suspect, often carrying too much baggage, weak and vulnerable, and very much dependent on grace and forgiveness.

The Good News is, He is gracious. He doesn't drive by on the other side of the road. He doesn't shrug his shoulders, saying "I would love to, but my car's already full". He is not fiddling in his glove compartment as he drives by. He doesn't ignore me. He stops for me. He offers me His help. He goes the extra mile for me. As I stand here and look up at that cross, I know he would go to hell and back for me. In fact, he already has.

Chapter 8

The Angel of Saint Calais

Saint Calais is even more deserted than Le Mans was when I left it early this morning. There is not a single person to be seen anywhere. As I walk the empty streets following the road signs in the direction of Orléans, I picture the tumbleweed blowing across the street just like in old western movies. I am tempted to look for a saloon but decide against it as I still have much ground to cover today.

I have to walk across to the outskirts of town on the eastern side, where I hope to have a better chance of getting a lift to Orléans. Every now and again I come across signs put up in people's gardens or on their fences, asking for a bypass to be built around the town in order to alleviate the amount of through traffic. I am all for the bypass. I wouldn't mind avoiding this place myself.

The road on the other side of town takes me up a long, steep hill. While walking, I hold my thumb out in the hitching position at the passing cars. Every now and again I turn around walking backwards and look into the cars in the hope that someone will take pity and stop for me.

Luxeuil-les-Bains, with its Columban monastery, is my next main port of call and lies directly east of Orléans. The blisters on my feet, and aching shoulders caused by the straps of the rucksack are not helping either. It has been tough going for the past two days. Progress has been slow. Frustratingly slow. I have even begun to question the whole venture, wondering to myself what I am doing here. This is after all my sabbatical. I am supposed to be taking it easy. Life in the ministry is stressful enough. That's why the church encourages its ministers to take time off. I could be at home now, relaxing on the patio, enjoying a cool drink with my wife. In fact, I can think of many things I could be doing right now that would be miles better than trudging my way through this French no-man's-land.

I have been walking uphill for the past hour in blistering heat and am feeling quite knackered, which is probably why at first I do not even notice a car stopping right beside me. I have also been deep in thought, trying to work out how long it would actually take me if I needed to walk the whole sixty mile stretch to Orléans. It is only when I see someone reaching across to unlock the front passenger door that I register what is happening. I look into the car and there she is, the angel of Saint Calais, struggling to open the passenger door of her Citroên ZX 1.9 Diesel.

Angels come in all shapes and sizes. This one is a petit brunette, called Pauline, about thirty years old, with long wavy hair tied up in a pony tail—stylish, and practical on a hot day like today. Pauline eventually gives up trying to unlock the passenger door from inside, and gets out to open it with her car key. She is wearing knee length jeans and a loose-fitting, white, collarless blouse. Both wrists and her left ankle are adorned with various bangles or bracelets made from leather or cotton, and she has a lit Marlboro cigarette in her right hand—well, not actually a genuine Marlboro—one of the cheap ones she bought in Egypt whilst on a recent scuba diving holiday—except that she didn't actually get scuba diving because a shark ate a German tourist the day before she arrived and all diving excursions were cancelled. I sense that Pauline is still miffed at that German tourist.

Pauline opens the boot of the car and tells me to throw my rucksack in. Looking into the boot my first thought is, where? Pauline's car is jam-packed with everything you can imagine and some things you wouldn't. Besides bags and cases and hold-alls, there is foodstuff, and clothes and towels, and all I can think of is the 1980's TV quiz show, 'The Generation Game', hosted by Bruce Forsyth, where the contestants sit at the conveyor belt and have to remember all the items that pass in front of them... fondue set, microwave oven, cuddly toy... "didn't they do well?"

Petite Pauline then grabs my rucksack and throws it onto the shelf behind the back seat. It just about fits in and with a bit of effort we get the boot closed. She then opens the passenger door and reaches in to clear away some stuff from the seat, simply tossing them over her shoulder into the back. It's only then that I notice a huge mattress, complete with sheet and duvet, folded and bunged into the back seats. How did I miss this? On the floor at the front passenger seat is a tray with twelve freshly baked buns... and a fifty Euro note. À toute vitesse the tray is lifted by Pauline and carefully balanced on the mattress behind our heads.

Settling into my seat, I notice the knob of the gear stick is covered by a bright orange tennis ball, and the side pocket of the passenger door is full of spanners, screwdrivers and various other technical gadgets. In fact there are probably more tools here than I have in my garage at home. As we set off, a bizarre thought goes through my head. I wonder what the forensic detectives of the TV Series CSI would make of our case if we were involved in a crash. One victim would have lost a lot of blood through lacerations to his thigh caused by a serrated blade similar to a hacksaw. The other victim seems to have choked on a chocolate fudge muffin, which would explain the significant residue of cake (with a tang of Egyptian tobacco) found at the scene. The whole crash scene is a total mess ... all, that is, except for a rucksack which, incredibly, is without a scratch, fully intact, as if it had been wrapped up in some kind of protective mattress-like material.

Tearing myself away from my bizarre thoughts and back to reality, I thank Pauline for giving me a lift. We engage in some small talk and she is surprised when I tell her I am a pastor, hitchhiking through Europe visiting medieval religious sites. It turns out she is on her way to Chamonix in the south east of France—nice for her, not so nice for me, because she will not be traveling through Orléans.

I am disappointed to hear this as I really could do with a bit of luck as far as the hitchhiking is concerned—my time schedule is already pretty tight. I open up my map to see what my options are and discover it is not as bad as I had feared. I can either get out at Epuisay, which is not far up the road, and try to make my way further east to Orléans. Or, if Pauline is happy with the idea, I could actually travel south east with her maybe even as far as Bourg-en-Bresse. This would be further south than I want to go, but I would be much closer to Luxeuil-les-Bains, my next destination.

Since we have known each other already for a full twenty minutes, I feel confident enough to ask Pauline what she thinks of the idea of me traveling with her all the way to Bourg-en-Bresse. I tell her I would be happy to share paying the motorway tolls with her.

"Mais, bien sûr", she replies, confirming my belief in angels, "No problem". Her answer means that we will spend the next six hours and three hundred and fifty-eight miles on the road together. Long enough to share a story or two.

After answering Pauline's many questions about myself, my profession and my family, I eventually get her to talk about herself. I discover that she is an extremely capable and accomplished young woman who seems to be able to put her hand to almost anything. I like her attitude, and her work ethic fascinates me. "I do not live to work", she tells me, "I work to live!". This, she explains, is the reason why she only works about eight months a year, and uses the rest of the time to travel.

When not traveling, she has various jobs. In a draper's, a butcher's and a bakery. She also does seasonal work like picking grapes or harvesting apples. She makes some of her own clothes, bakes with a passion, and loves arts and crafts. All the jewellery she is wearing is self-made, and she even repairs her own car, which is why she loves her twenty year old Citroên with its 230,000 miles on the clock! I do hope she has changed the timing belt... at least twice.

Although she has quite an unorthodox take on life and work, Pauline has, as we would say in Belfast, her feet firmly on the ground and her head well screwed onto her shoulders. She is intelligent, self-assured and has obviously benefited from her world travels. She is just back from four months hitchhiking through Asia, making and selling her own trinkets and jewellery to get by, whenever her finances were getting low.

"That's why I stopped for you", she says, "I know what it's like on the road."

"I am glad you stopped", I reply, "I have already walked about ten miles today and was beginning to give up hope."

"How heavy is your rucksack?"

"About twelve kilos—I think I have too much stuff with me."

"*Oh certainement!* You really only need eight kilos at the most for your trip. My rucksack weighed twenty kilos when I was in Asia, but I was traveling for four months. And I was still usually walking about twenty miles a day, but only ten in the mountains."

"Only ten?!", I think to myself, feeling my self-esteem take a knock. I don't say it out loud, but *je suis déprimé.*

Not for long however. We are soon making our way southeast through the breathtaking region of Bourgogne with its impressive sunflower fields as we follow the River Loire and its tributaries through Blois to Macon. Simply stunning. I make a mental note to come back here on holiday. Preferably with a bike, or a boat, or both.

We don't really have time to take a proper break, because Pauline wants to be in Chamonix by midnight, so we make a brief stop at a service station to buy some sandwiches and drinks. I discreetly buy a packet of cigarettes to give my driver as a little thank you. Marlboro. The real ones.

The timing belt of the little Citroên has done its job well and we arrive in Bourg-en-Bresse at around nine o'clock. The angel of Saint Calais goes out of her way to drop me off in the town centre, where I will have a better chance of finding a bed for the night. I thank her for her kindness, handing over the Marlboro, and wishing her God's blessing on her life. Then, as quickly as she appeared, she is gone, the little black ZX 1.9 Diesel disappearing into the night traffic heading back out of town, Chamonix bound.

As I walk into the town centre, I can't help thinking about the past few hours on the road with the angel of Saint Calais. I shake my head in disbelief as I think about how I did not notice that huge mattress stuffed diagonally across the back seats of the car. I think of the tray of home baked buns with a fifty Euro note balancing on top. I think of our topics of conversation: politics, travel, education, philosophy, church, faith, God, life, society, marriage and family.

I also learned today that to tell someone to shut their mouth in French is even more rude than using a swear word. And I laugh out loud as I remember that today I also learned the French word for 'orgy'! By accident, I might add. It was just one of those funny lost-in-translation moments as I was searching for the French word for 'everywhere'. I think about that stunningly beautiful route through the Bourgogne, and my wish to holiday here. I think of this petit Power-Frau that exudes confidence with her can-do attitude, and all she has accomplished and achieved. The countries she has visited, the adventures she has been on.

And then I remember something she said today, almost in passing, and yet incredibly poignant: "It would be nice to have someone to share it all with. Someone to travel the world with." Ironically, Pauline is not alone, at least not in this regard. How many others long for exactly the same thing? A partner to do life together with. Someone to journey with. To make plans with. To decide routes and share loads with. Even Columbanus didn't travel alone. He had his twelve friends with whom he shared life.

As I think about Pauline's words I am reminded of God's words to Adam before He created Eve: "It is not good to be alone." I guess not. Not even in paradise. And the majestic sunflowers we passed en route today, standing shoulder to shoulder in the warm Bourgogne sun, would seem to agree.

Chapter 9

Creeds, Confessions and Other Contradictions

I need to find accommodation for the night and I also wouldn't mind looking at my maps and planning my route for tomorrow. If I had been better organised, I could probably have found a couch to sleep on over the couch surfing website that I have signed up to for this trip. But the hitchhiking makes it almost impossible to say with certainty where you will be come nightfall. There was no way that I could have foreseen that I would be in Bourg-en-Bresse tonight.

I take a seat at one of the tables outside a quaint little café in the town centre in order to gather my thoughts and consider my plan of action. It is just after nine o'clock—plenty of time to sort accommodation. A young couple are sitting at the table beside me. Otherwise, the café seems to be pretty much unoccupied. The young man, who turns out to be the owner of the café, immediately gets up and comes over to me. *"Bonsoir, Monsieur. Vous désirez?"* Indeed I do, I think to myself, and answer, *"Bonsoir. Je voudrais un coca, s'il vous plait."*

When he returns with my coke, I already have my map spread out across the table, working out how best to get to Luxeuil-les-Bains tomorrow. As there is nothing else much happening in the café, the young owner sits down again with his fiancé at the table next to me. I use the opportunity to ask him if he can recommend me a cheap bed and breakfast for the night. When he answers me in English, I wonder if it is because my French is so bad, or because he just wants to practise his English.

"There is an inexpensive guesthouse nearby. I can phone and make a reservation for you if you want.", he offers. His English obviously doesn't need practising, but I nevertheless decide not to continue this conversation in French. "That would be great. Thanks a lot."

My accommodation now sorted, I turn my attention to tomorrow's route. Claude—we are now on first name terms—offers to assist. He uses an app on his smartphone to show me the best way to get to the outskirts of the city. From here I plan to head for Besançon, and then further north to Luxeuil.

Claude's fiancé has been joined by two of her friends, so the young man joins me at my table. He is interested to hear more about my pilgrimage following the trail of Saint Columbanus through Europe. I order us two drinks and we are soon engaged in deep conversation, interrupted only when Claude has to serve a customer, in other words his fiancé and her two friends.

I am not surprised by how open my new French friend is, nor by how willing he is to talk about spiritual things. This has often been my experience when I meet people outside church circles, even in the comparatively atheistic setting of eastern Germany. When people hear that I am a pastor and theologian, they quite often want to talk about some personal issue they are dealing with, or ask some questions pertaining to matters of faith. Despite what one is led to believe, there is very much an openness and indeed hunger for spirituality in society today. Just because people are not interested in our church services does not mean they are not spiritual. This can sometimes be difficult for church folk like myself to accept, but it doesn't make it any less true.

The conversations I have had with the various people I've encountered on my Columban travels have been no exception. People have talked with me about their mistakes in life and the deep feelings of remorse and guilt that still paralyse them today. They have trusted me enough to tell me of the hurts they have experienced, some of them at the hands of Christians or the church. They have shared their deeply held opinions about their beliefs and their values. They have questioned me on almost every aspect of my Christian faith. And many of them were glad for me to pray with or for them.

Most of the time I just listen to the people, let them talk. I say just listen, when in fact listening is actually one of the most important things to do. It also happens to be one of the most difficult things to do—to listen, intently, also to what is not being said—at least not verbally—without judging, without interrupting, without always wanting to tell the person what you think or what they should do.

Of course, sometimes people have asked me why I believe in God, or to explain a particular aspect of my faith. My answers are many and various, depending on the person, the context and the mood I am in. For instance, when asked why I believe in God, I might mischievously answer, "Because He believes in me". And it's true. He does believe in me. When all others are ready to give up on me, and sometimes rightly so, God believes in me. He has faith in me. He doesn't dump me, even when He has cause to. Not ever. Tell me that isn't good news.

When you start to grasp this, it is difficult not to believe in Him. Likewise, if you truly understand and experience God's offer of forgiveness for yesterday, strength for today and hope for tomorrow, it is difficult not to believe in Him. Or if you have clearly heard the Maker of the universe whisper into your ear, "I made you. I love you. I have a wonderful plan for you. Let's do life together", it's difficult not to believe in Him. If you have personally experienced how His love has totally transformed your life for the better—not necessarily easier, but better—it is also difficult not to believe in Him.

Now I know that is a lot of 'ifs', but that is exactly why I love my job. I find it fascinating and rewarding helping people make some sense of all those 'ifs'. Naturally, I too have my doubts, and sometimes more questions than answers. In fact, I actually believe that there is much about God that will probably never make sense, at least not this side of eternity. As a better man than me once said, "Si comprehendis, non est Deus" ('If you understand it, it ain't God'—St. Augustine).

I think the apostle Paul describes it well in the Bible when he talks about us not being able to see clearly in this world. Paul says it's as if we are looking through frosted glass where we can't really focus on any objects clearly. Maybe it's like a spiritual version of the greenhouse effect where our world is so full of mess that the windows are all steamed up making it impossible to see out, to see God, to see what's actually important in life. Or like the very first time I got my eyes tested and started wearing new glasses. I hadn't realised that up until then I had been looking at the world through a polythene bag!

If the apostle Paul is right, the day will come when all humanity will stand before God and see all things as they really are—clearly, truly.

If you are struggling with this biblical concept, you may find the Hollywood version more helpful. Think of Neo, played by Keanu Reeves in 'The Matrix' movie, when Morpheus presents him with a choice of the red pill or the blue pill. Only if Neo chooses to swallow the red pill, will he be able to see the Matrix and understand his world as it really is. Only then will things make sense. In this analogy the apostle Paul is like Morpheus. The red pill that opens our eyes is equivalent to standing before God in heaven at the end of time when all will be revealed. There, our eyes will be opened and all things will make sense. And let's face it, that has to be a good thing because from down here a lot of things don't make sense at all. I guess that's why I get asked so many questions:

Does God exist? Can you prove that God exists? Why does He not just come back today and do some amazing miracle to convince everyone that He exists? Is there really a heaven? Is there really a hell? Who is going to hell? Who is going to heaven? Is Ghandi in heaven? Is Judas in heaven? Is Hitler in heaven? How can heaven be perfect, if you know there are people in hell? Do you think you will be able to party away in heaven, knowing that there are millions suffering eternal torment in hell? How can that be paradise?

Can't I just believe in God and not go to church? Is the church as we have it today really what Jesus had in mind? If there is a God, why does He allow suffering in the world? Does God predestine everything? Would we not be better off without religion—look at all the wars in the world that are caused by religion?

Which religion is the right one? How do you know you are right? Is not all truth relative? How can you believe in an absolute truth? What about the cruelty and suffering that has been done in the name of God and religion—the crusades, the inquisition, the missions in colonial times, paedophile priests, the grave moral shortcomings of hypocritical Christian leaders?

Would it not be better to sell all the church's riches and give the money to the poor? What would Jesus do? How do you reconcile the apparent contradictions in the Bible? Do you really believe the universe was made in six days? What happened to the dinosaurs? How did Noah get all the animals into his ark? Why didn't he leave the mosquitoes behind? Why did God even make mosquitoes in the first place? Did Adam really name all the animals? Was God drunk when He designed the zebra? Or does God just have it in for zebras? I mean, what chance does a zebra have to mingle discreetly into its natural habitat in order to avoid being eaten by a lion?!

Who did Adam and Eve's sons marry? Was that really God in the manger in Bethlehem in the Christmas story? Are God, Jesus and the Holy Spirit really all one person? How does that work? Did Jesus really walk on water? Was Mary really a virgin? (wink wink, nudge nudge) Did Jesus really turn water into wine? ... and why don't preachers repeat this? The churches would be full! No pun intended.

Did Jesus really feed five thousand people with just five loaves and two fish? Why did Jesus stick his fingers into the deaf mute's ears in order to heal him? And why did he take spittle from his mouth and use it to touch this man's mouth in order to make him able to speak again? Did Jesus have to do such weird things at all? Surely he could just have healed this deaf mute without all the sticky finger stuff? Why did he not just raise his hand and speak the words, "Be healed!"? He did on other occasions—why not here? And if he had to do this weird stuff at all, why not at least do the tongue touching before the ear touching?!

On and on the questions go—some of them trivial, many of them not. Why are some people healed and others not? What are we here for? Why do bad things happen to good people? If there is a God, why does He not hear my prayer? How does prayer work, anyway? Does God have to be begged by us before He lifts a finger? Does prayer make God change His mind? Why does a good God have to be asked at all? Surely He should know what I need, even before I ask? Does He wait until a certain number of prayers are offered up before He acts? And what if I don't manage to pray enough? Does God not act because I just happen to fall, say, two prayers short of His minimum prayer requirement?

And what's this whole thing about the cross? Why should something that happened two thousand years ago on the other side of the world have anything at all to do with me today? Why did Jesus have to die on the cross for me at all—I don't want His blood on my hands? Anyway, what kind of God requires the shedding of blood in order to forgive? Can

God not just forgive me without requiring that His son dies a painful death in the process? And what is happening at Holy Communion? Do Christians really eat and drink the body and blood of Christ?

And what about the Old Testament—have you read some of the crazy stuff you find in there? It doesn't get much better when you read some of the bizarre and ridiculous stories of Saint Columbanus and his companions in the church of the Middle Ages.

Then there are the other questions that people ask about the life of faith. These questions are somewhat different and belong to another category, but they are similar in that they are asked because people are truly baffled by what they read, see or hear. It makes no sense to them:

You Christians are different. Why do you behave differently? What harm is there in a little white lie? Everyone is doing it, why not you? What's the big deal? Does the Bible really say "Love your enemies and do good to those that hate you"? Where will that get you in this life? What did Jesus mean when he said "Whoever seeks to save his life must lose it for my sake"? How can a life of self-sacrifice be life in all its fullness. Where is the logic in that? Did Jesus really say, "I have not come into the world to condemn the world, but to save it."? You wouldn't think that, when you talk to some of the Christians I know!

Did Jesus really reach out the hand of healing and friendship to lepers, enemy Roman soldiers, the hated tax collectors, prostitutes, adulterers, foreigners and immigrants, thieves and outcasts? Did he really cross social, cultural, economic and religious boundaries to show people what the God of love is truly like? And what did he mean when he said

"If anyone is thirsty, let him come to me and drink"? Really? How? Can you help me understand this man who seems to have satisfied the thirst and so transformed the lives of billions of people down through the centuries?

This last question is actually a very shrewd one. I never cease to be amazed at people who say they are atheists, although they have never seriously looked at the material. Either they have never bothered to read the Scriptures at all, or they have a selective understanding of church history, or they have only "read" Christians, who it must be said are often a poor reflection of their master. My somewhat cheeky response to them is usually something along the lines of, "I'm sorry, but you don't know enough to be an atheist. You need to find out about the thing you are rejecting in order to know what you are rejecting!" To me this is just common sense.

That is why I often challenge or encourage people to educate themselves about the Christian faith so that they can make an informed decision about accepting or rejecting it. Making a decision on anything important in life, without having the right information, or even worse, having the wrong information, is not only ridiculous, but stupid.

It has been fascinating chatting with Claude, but it is almost eleven o'clock and I need to make tracks. I say my goodbyes, promising to send him a postcard from the monastery at Luxeuil, and make my way up the hill to the B&B where I will stay the night. It is near the train and bus station, about ten minutes walk from the café. The small bar downstairs is still open, but after checking in I make my way upstairs to my room which justifies its price—cheap. After a quick shower to cool down I read a few pages of John's gospel before falling into bed with the music from the bar filtering up through the bedroom floor. Snow Patrol's frontman, Gary Lightbody, another one of Bangor's famous sons, is singing "Chasing Cars".

I smile at the irony of it. Nice one, God.

Chapter 10

The French Connection

I am wakened at six o'clock by a dawn chorus of the fleet of buses warming up their engines directly outside my window in preparation for their first tour of the day. Even though I was aware that the bus and train terminals were nearby, I had left the window opened last night due to the unbearable heat. The ear plugs I was wearing were useless. I might as well have been lying on a bed on the tarmac in the middle of the bus terminal. It would not have been any noisier.

My room, a *chambre confortable*, cost ten Euros more than the *chambre simple*, which were all booked up when I asked last night (yeah, sure). My chamber is anything but comfortable. I get up, close the windows, readjust the earplugs and manage to sleep until eight.

As breakfast is not included in my room deal, I walk across the street to a little *boulangerie* for a croissant and a cup of tea. They also have internet access so I manage to send a couple of last minute requests for a couch for the night in Luxeuil, where I plan to be tonight. It's a long shot and I will have to keep checking into the website throughout the day to see how my requests are doing, but it's worth a try.

In a small *supermarché* I buy a bottle of water, a pasta

mix and some chocolate. Following Claude's route from the night before, I make my way to the outskirts of town and the A39 which will take me to Besançon. As I walk, I have my thumb held out to the approaching motorists. I smile again, as I think of "Chasing Cars", God's lullaby to me last night. How many will I chase today, I wonder.

I hear the next car approaching from behind me, but I deliberately keep walking without turning around. In the psychology of hitchhiking I call this the the priming zone. I am talking here about the vitally important three to five seconds just before interaction between hiker and motorist. It is a safe zone because there is not yet any contact. The hiker is not facing the driver. There is no eye-contact, no request, no direct interaction. Driver and hiker are both still safe in their own little worlds.

But these few brief seconds also serve to prime the motorist for a possible transaction. Consciously, and subconsciously, the sight of a hitchhiker with a backpack walking along the side of the road has an effect on an approaching motorist. The powers of suggestion are at work where the hitchhiker communicates a message without even speaking a word, the backpack basically saying it all for him. In these few seconds the motorist is indirectly being asked to consider the possibility of stopping or at the very least, he or she is being readied for the formal request which then comes with the outstretched thumb.

I hear the car behind me getting closer, close enough to switch to the next phase of the process, the request. I turn to face the silver Toyota Avensis, making its way up the hill towards me. I wait until I can almost see the whites of the driver's eyes before pulling the trigger, or rather, sticking my thumb out. I keep walking backwards and looking the driver in the face, but not in the eye, giving him or her the chance to make that split second decision to stop for me. The decision does not go my way and the Toyota drives on past. As do the next seven vehicles. But then my luck changes, big time.

An Opel Vectra pulls over and the driver, a middle-aged man, opens the front passenger door for me. I am delighted when I discover that he is on his way to visit his daughter who lives in Vesoul, just fifteen miles from Luxeuil. A further two uneventful lifts later and I am finally in the town of Luxeuil-les-Bains, which in the closing years of the sixth century was basically 'Columbanus World'.

Here in this Vosges region of France, Columbanus would establish three monasteries, the most influential of which would be built on the ruins of a Roman town which had been destroyed in 451 by Attila the Hun. The Roman name of the town was Luxovian, or Luxeuil in Columbanus' day, and today the spa town Luxeuil-les Bains. Throughout the opening decades of the 7th century, thousands of monks would emerge from these Luxovien monasteries with a missionary spirit that would quite literally change the religious and political landscape of Europe of the Middle Ages.

How was this possible? How were the Bangor monks able to set up such significant monastic settlements? And why were they so successful, not only in France, but also in the regions we know today as Germany, Austria, Switzerland and Italy?

Faith minded people may like to describe it as God's providence, a so-called *Kairos* (timely) moment in history, when God looks especially favourably on His servants. Others might simply see the political powers of the day at work. Either way, it meant that the Frankish King Childebert II of Austrasien (the present day border region between France and Germany) donated land to Columbanus and invited him to set up shop in his neighbourhood.

A clever move as it turns out, because this enabled the Franks to emancipate themselves from the ruling bishops of their day. These bishops were a legacy of the Roman empire and still had the say not only on religious matters, but also politically. The Irish monks were not a part of the Roman structures, celtic Christianity developing independently from the Roman empire with its strict hierarchical structures.

The missionary monks from Bangor therefore did things differently. In celtic Christianity the abbot had the say, not the bishop. The Bangor monks were loyal and obedient first and foremost to their abbot (Columbanus), and not to any local bishop. This Irish understanding of monastic life and rule suited the Frankish nobility, who were glad to break free from the Roman set up. They gladly sent their sons to Columbanus to be educated or indeed trained to take on holy orders. Many of them later became bishops or founded their own monasteries, so that by the middle of the seventh century there were over 300 new Columban monasteries in northern France alone. This missionary zeal continued into the eighth century with further prominent monasteries being founded in Germany, Austria and Switzerland.

Monsieur Opel Vectra drops me off in the centre of Luxeuil right beside *Saint Columban Lingerie*, a shop selling, as you might imagine, lingerie and dessous. How times have changed. One minute you are the spiritual leader of an influential monastic movement that is changing the world, the next you are selling French knickers on the high street. I can't help wondering what Columbanus would think if he were around today. When I see the scary statue of him situated directly outside the main entrance to the abbey, I get my answer.

An angry Columbanus, standing with staff raised, in a threatening posture on top of a tall marble base, is looking menacingly down at me. The statue depicts his outrage at the immoral lifestyle of Theuderich II, the King of Burgundy, who obviously saw more than his fair share of French knickers. Full marks to Columbanus for being true to his principles, even when it meant criticizing the powers that be. I can't help thinking, however, that this statue is not exactly the most inviting image to have situated at the entrance to your church.

The magnificent abbey church of Saint-Columban, known today as the basilica of Saint Peter and Saint Paul, is still the heart and soul of the town that grew up around it in 590. It has been rebuilt on a number of occasions, having suffered attacks from the Vandals in the 8th century, the Normans in the 9th century and the Hungarians in the 10th century. Even the French themselves had a go at it during the French Revolution, expelling the monks, burning the treasured books of its magnificent library and using its hallowed cloisters as a covered market. The revolutionaries did however leave the buildings in tact, the oldest parts of which date back to the 13th century.

I decide not to go into the abbey just yet. I will have plenty of time for that over the next few days. My priority right now is to find accommodation for the night. I use my phone to check the couch surfing website for any possible answers to the requests I sent this morning. Negative. In preparing for this trip I had read that it is possible for pilgrims to stay in the monastery, so I make my way round to the office. Unfortunately the office is closed, with no sign of life anywhere.

I walk across the street to the tourist information office and enquire about accommodation in the monastery. They are just about to close up shop for the day, but the helpful Madame there makes time for me and confirms that men (yes, only men) on a *pélerinage* (pilgrimage) are indeed able to stay in the abbey. She even phones the director for me, but is only able to leave a message on the answer machine. She then suggests that I walk around to the back of the building where there is another entrance. Perhaps I will be able to reach someone there. Perhaps.

Following the good lady's advice I pilgrim my way back across the street to the monastery, looking for the rear entrance. This is not quite as easy as it may sound as the abbey site, complete with church, extensive gardens, art gallery, and accommodation block, is huge. I try to keep the high walls of the monastery in sight, using them as a means of orientation as I pass through the quaint little side streets skirting the abbey until I come to large blue gates facing out onto *Rue Henry Guy*.

The sign, *Abbaye Saint Columban*, lets me know I am at the right place. Unfortunately for me, the sign also says *Fermeture des portes à tout moment*, which explains why I am standing in front of closed and locked gates. I search around for a door bell or some kind of intercom that might give me access to the monastery but find nothing.

I am beginning to understand the later Benedictine influence on this abbey, with its high walls, cloisters and locked doors sheltering its monks' ascetic life from the world outside. celtic monastic settlements, on the other hand, were never established as a means to withdraw from the world in seclusion, but rather to be among the people, to reach out and serve those around them. This is why celtic monastic settlements were established near main roads and trade routes, in places people frequented, not in the back end of nowhere.

Back in the 6th century when this place was a celtic monastic settlement under Columbanus' rule, it was open to all, a centre of learning, a place of refuge, a place of work and a spiritual home to many. I find it frustrating to have come so far and to be actually standing right in front of the monastery, facing high walls and locked gates which prevent me entering.

It is getting late and I am just starting to become a little concerned about my sleeping arrangements for tonight when I notice the name of the street directly opposite me, *Rue Saint-Columban*. This name sounds familiar to me, reminding me of the list of contacts that my old friend on Bangor City Council gave me before I set out on my journey. I set my rucksack down and open up the side pocket where I keep my passport, a credit card and my list of VIPs. There, under Luxeuil-les-Bains, I find the name Jacques Dupont, president of the Luxeuil branch of the 'Friends of Saint Columbanus', who, *quelle surprise*, just happens to live on the street Rue Saint Columban.

The first thing I notice about Monsieur Dupont's place is its impressive garden—well kept, whilst maintaining that natural look which complements the house itself, a detached villa with loads of character and charm. The antique doorbell pull, dating back to the early twentieth century, suggests to me that this is not the house that Jacques built.

When Jacques Dupont opens the door and greets me with a friendly *Bonsoir Monsieur* I introduce myself *en français*. I then explain where I come from and what I am doing—that I am on a *pélerinage* in the footsteps of Saint Columbanus and that I can't get into the abbey because the gates are *fermé*. Jacques invites me into his home and introduces me to his wife. I gladly accept their offer of a cool drink while Jacques makes a simple phone call and arranges accommodation for me in the monastery. No sooner said than done.

When we head back down the road in Jacques' car, the big blue gates are already open and we drive unhindered into the expansive grounds of the monastery. Inside, the driveway skirts around the large manicured lawns up to the main entrance where I am told a monk will meet me and show me to my room.

I am a little nervous about meeting this monk, mainly because I have never met a monk before. At least not a real one. I did meet one at a fancy dress party a few years back but that doesn't really count, does it? To put it blankly, Northern Ireland Protestants don't really do monks. Monks, like saints, tend on the whole to be a Catholic thing. For this reason I am not quite sure what to expect.

A part of me is expecting to be met by a thirty-something year old man, a quiet contemplative type, complete with the traditional monk uniform of habit and rope belt. Another part of me is expecting a well-rounded, jovial type à la Friar

Tuck out of a Robin Hood movie. I am a little surprised then, when Jacques' car pulls up at the main entrance and we are greeted by a man, aged about 70, wearing dark trousers and a short sleeved, checked shirt. Well, at least he is wearing Jesus sandals.

I am delighted to be meeting my first ever monk. Shaking hands with him, I introduce myself in French and begin to thank him for the offer of accommodation in the monastery. When I am finished talking, this dear old monk smiles at me and takes me totally by surprise when he speaks to me in English with a rich Dublin brogue. "This sounds to me like a person from the North making a miserable attempt to speak French." I know I am in France, and I know I am at a Columban monastery, but I was just not expecting to be welcomed here by Frère Jacques and a monk from Dublin called Patrick!

Amazing. Just like the next four days I will spend here in this mystical place.

Chapter 11

Home Alone

P atrick leads me by flashlight to my room, through long dark corridors adorned with oil paintings and grand statues of Saint Columbanus and other such venerables. The monastery is huge—not to mention quite spooky in the dark. It doesn't help matters when Patrick proceeds to tell me that we are the only two people staying in the monastery this weekend. During term time the abbey, which now functions as a public school, would be buzzing with children, but it's summer and the kids are all on school holidays. There are a few other monks and a general manager who would also normally be here, but it just so happens that they all are away for this weekend. We are here all alone—just the two of us. This information takes me quite by surprise. It won't be the last time Patrick surprises me this evening.

Following in the shadows behind Patrick, with his torch in one hand and a big bunch of keys jingling in the other, I try not to freak out thinking about spending the night alone here in this historic monastery. I know it is silly, but I can't help thinking of Hogwarts, the school for wizards from the Harry Potter books. Thankfully I only have fifteen minutes to get changed before Jacques calls to pick us up again. He has invited Patrick and me to his house for supper.

Madame Dupont has prepared a lovely meal for us consisting of quiche, a mixed salad with delicious home grown tomatoes from the garden, and a crusty baguette—the continental version of the Belfast bap. In typically French fashion, we complement our meal with a nice bottle of *vin rouge* and a selection of cheeses, my favourite being the extremely pungent *Epoisses*.

The temperature has cooled down to a comfortable 23 degrees Celsius as we sit on the patio late into the evening enjoying good food and each other's company. As the Duponts do not speak English, the conversation takes place in French. Patrick is fluent in French and English, both with a Dublin accent, and I am so glad of his help in translating complicated phrases.

Jacques, as one might expect of the president of the local branch of the 'Friends of Saint Columbanus', is a walking encyclopaedia on both Saint Columbanus and Luxeuil. His study is full of books and literature on the Irish saint and the history of the abbey. He has been to all the historic sites on the Columbanus trail, including a visit to Bangor Abbey, and he knows most of the key people involved in the "Friends" network at European level.

His interest in Saint Columbanus is by no means merely academic. For Jacques it is a passion, and he is obviously delighted as I pose question after question, his eyes lighting up as he talks. My amazement at Jacques' vast pool of knowledge on the subject is just slightly greater than my amazement at how much French I actually understand.

Having had a wonderful evening with Madame *et* Monsieur Dupont, Patrick and I make our way back down the road to the monastery. Just before reaching the grand blue gates, which again stand closed before us, Patrick takes out a little remote control from his pocket, points it in the direction of the gates and they begin to open automatically. I am impressed. Saint Columbanus was used to getting wild animals to obey him, which makes me think that getting a gate to open without touching it would have impressed him too.

Once inside the cloister we stop and wait until the gates are fully closed before walking to the main building. It has been a long day and although I have had a delightful evening, conversing in French has been exhausting. I am glad that Patrick speaks to me in English. All the more so when he surprises me for the second time tonight with, "Do you take a drink?"

"What do you mean?"

"Would you like a whiskey? I have an unopened bottle of Jameson that I've had for ages, if you fancy a nightcap."

Even though I know that Jacques is picking us up early tomorrow morning to take us on a tour of some of the main historical sites, I can't resist Patrick's kind offer. I sense he would enjoy the company, and to be honest, a part of me is pleased to delay being home alone in my room in a remote corner of Hogwarts castle.

Sitting down at the kitchen table, Patrick blows the dust off his bottle of whiskey, opens it and pours a measure into my glass. I am adding some water to my whiskey when I see Patrick putting the bottle away in the cupboard again. "Aren't you having any?", I ask him. Then Patrick completes his hattrick. For a third time tonight he totally surprises me. "Oh no, I don't touch the stuff. I am a recovering alcoholic. I haven't touched a drop in years."

I now understand why he did not have a glass of wine tonight at Jacques, but I still feel uncomfortable and begin to object that I should not be drinking alcohol in his company. He assures me that this is absolutely no problem and insists that I continue drinking my whiskey. Sipping on his lemonade, Patrick begins to tell me how his alcohol problems started. His is an interesting story.

Patrick is what is known in the Roman Catholic church as a Columban Father, a missionary in Saint Columban's Foreign Missionary Society. This non-profit society was set up in 1916 by two young Irish priests who had a burden for the multitudes of Chinese people who still had not heard of God's love for them. Today there are over 600 Columban missionaries striving for social justice and peace in some of the world's poorest communities.

After training for the priesthood in Maynooth, Dublin, Patrick was sent as a Columban missionary to the Philippines, where he helped establish a social outreach centre. Over the next thirty years, Patrick's mission work would take him to over one hundred countries, and he would serve in some of the most difficult and dangerous situations in Asia. By far the worst time of his ministry was the day he witnessed a fellow Columban priest, and good friend, being kidnapped in Burma. The priest was never found again.

A part of Patrick also died that day. He fell into depression and starting drinking heavily in a futile search to ease the pain. Thankfully, his superiors were there to help. He was allowed time off and given therapy to help him work through his grief, enabling him to return to work and serve the church for many more years.

Sipping on our drinks, Patrick and I exchange stories

and questions on all manner of subjects. We are keen to hear each others take on Irish history or various theological topics. He helps me understand the structures of the Roman Catholic church, and I explain to him the structures of the Methodist Church. Even when we don't agree with each other's point of view, we agree to disagree. Patrick also helps me fill in the blanks on the subject of Columbanus and the work of the Bangor monks here in Luxeuil, whilst constantly adding, "But you'll see all that tomorrow."

I can't quite believe I am sitting in Columbanus' abbey in Luxeuil, in the most enjoyable company of an Irish Columban priest, conversing about mission, both medieval and modern day. It might not be everyone's cup of tea, but I wonder if it gets any better than this. I shouldn't wonder. As Patrick repeatedly said, "You'll see all that tomorrow."

Chapter 12

A Thin Place

I am wakened at dawn by strange noises I cannot quite place. They are muffled and indistinct, but sound to me a bit like a monk engaged in some kind of chanting in the room above mine. Lying in my bed in the dark my imagination starts to run riot. What if Patrick and I are not the only ones here? What if there is someone else here, some old monk who has lost his marbles and is kept hidden from sight up in the attic of the monastery? I soon have warped pictures in my mind of a deranged monk like Silas, from the movie 'The Da Vinci Code', flagellating himself in an ecstatic rant in the room above me.

Pulling myself together, I get up and open the wooden shutters in my room. It is amazing the difference a little light makes. It always is. The ecstatic rants of my deranged monk locked up in the attic turn out to be nothing more than a couple of pigeons cooing on the rooftop above my window. Not knowing whether to laugh or be annoyed at my own silliness, I fall into bed and drift back to sleep. But not for long. I am wakened by the church bells ringing at 7 a.m. For some reason they ring seven times at seven o'clock, another seven times at 7.02 and then three times thrice at 7.05. I take the hint and stumble out of bed and into the day.

After a shower and a shave I am sufficiently awake to take in my new surroundings. My guest room is typical for a monastery—plain, simple, sufficient. The only article that is not of obvious practical purpose is a small wooden icon image of Christ hanging on the wall above my bed. The windows are floor to ceiling like patio doors and are held closed by means of a vertical iron bar locking system. Simple folding wooden panel shutters on the inside render curtains unnecessary.

My room overlooks the courtyard with its dominant centrepiece, an imposing bronze statue of *Columban d'Irlande*. The ivy that has grown around the base and up over Columbanus' shoulder suits him well. The saint from Bangor now stands in a sea of green wearing a sash over his shoulder.

His left arm is outstretched to bless the land, but during the Second World War the Nazis chose to interpret this outstretched arm differently. They occupied this town in 1941, glad of its small airfield nearby, and used the famous old library block of the abbey as a training school for pilots. They claimed that Columbanus' statue with the outstretched arm did not depict him blessing the land but instead shows him doing the Nazi salute. There is some similarity and I can imagine the jokes that must surely have been made each time a new commandant arrived at the monastery for the first time. When I was growing up, I remember seeing comedians do the Hitler salute in shows on TV. As children we would sometimes copy them on the playground, clicking our heels together and raising our outstretched palm in the air. Just a bit of fun really. Or so we thought. Germans today find nothing humorous about the so-called Hitler salute. Doing it today can even lead to prosecution. Rightly so, when you think about it.

After breakfast I meet Patrick and Jacques who have kindly offered to give me a guided tour of the area and all things Columbanus. We drive about ten miles east of Luxeuil to Annegray where the Bangor monks set up their first monastic settlement on the remains of an old Roman military fort. King Guntram was only too glad to offer Columbanus this land and have the renowned scholarly Irish monks stay in his kingdom. They would help bring order out of the chaos that was the order of the day.

Back in the late sixth century this region was still mainly heathen. Roman Christianity had taken root in the larger towns, but for various reasons the Church had mostly lost its way. Corruption and immorality among clergy were not uncommon. "The creed alone remained", was how Jonas, the seventh century biographer of Columbanus, described the spiritual climate of the region.

Creeds are important, but so too are deeds. This was where Columbanus and the Bangor missionaries excelled. Their form of celtic monasticism, with its equal emphasis on the development of body, mind and spirit, ensured that the new monastic settlements in the Vosges mountains would not only be centres of discipleship and spirituality but also of education and culture. Unlike many modern day expressions of faith, the dichotomy between the sacred and the secular did not exist in celtic monasticism. The celtic way of deep personal piety along with an honest work ethic, would renew hearts and minds, and transform community life as a whole.

The Bangor monks were indeed saints and scholars. They had benefited from the fact that Ireland never suffered the barbarian invasions that had so decimated the libraries of continental Europe. Students came to Ireland from as far away as Egypt in order to attend the renowned Irish centres of learning. Columbanus and his colleagues enjoyed the vast resources of celtic Christian culture and literature, as well as classical learning in the arts and sciences available to them in Bangor. Whilst Pope Gregory the Great was forbidding Greek, banishing the Mathematicians from Rome and denouncing learning, the Irish monks were thriving on becoming some of the best scholars in the western world.

They were masters in the scriptures, transcribing their own copies by hand. They were knowledgeable in the sciences, gifted in writing poetry, story-telling and hymnody, but they also had important practical skills in areas such as carpentry, pottery, medicine, ironmongery, weaving and farming. To put it in today's terms they had a great *curriculum vitae* (including speaking Latin, by the way) and would be an asset to any company. It's no wonder King Guntram was so keen to have them stay.

We are surrounded on all sides by forested hills as Jacques parks in front of a quaint little church on a quiet country road. On a hill about a mile to the north is the little church of Saint Martin, from where we have just come. From *L'Eglise Saint Martin* we had a bird's eye view of where we are now standing, Columbanus' first monastic site at Annegray.

The other notable thing about Saint Martin's church on the hill is the engraving of a cross in its stonework. The cross itself is not that remarkable, but the two celtic symbols engraved either side of it are a surprising reminder that, although in France, this site was once a main centre of Irish monasticism and a significant nursery of celtic Christian mission in Europe. Jacques tells me that the engraved stone—which is obviously much older than the other ones used to build the chapel—dates back to the early Middle Ages when Irish influence shaped the region.

Getting out of the car, I am able to read the name of the small chapel before us—*Saint- Jean-Baptiste-D'Annegray*. The church, being almost as broad as it is long, has a cube-like form with an elegant pyramid shaped roof which apexes to a forged iron cross complete with weathervane cockerel. The first weathervanes were usually in the form of Triton, a Greek sea-god, but when the Roman empire became Christian the cockerel became the prominent symbol on weathervanes. This was to signify the humility of Saint Peter who, as Jesus had predicted, denied Christ three times before the cockerel crowed twice.

I notice the ornamental niche built into the stonework directly above the main door and Jacques tells me that until recently, a small statue of John the Baptist was on display there. That is, until someone stole him. It beggars belief. Jacques then takes out a bunch of keys and lets us into the church.

The first things I notice inside are the two statues of Saint Columbanus and Saint John the Baptist each with their own small metal plaque dating them in the 17th century. Besides various religious paintings, the walls are also adorned with two busts, one of Saint Columbanus and one of Saint Valbert, the third abbot of Luxeuil. Each bust contains a small glass display cabinet containing pieces of bone. Relics of the two Luxeuil abbots. I am no expert, but I reckon I am looking at Valbert's thigh bone and two pieces of Columbanus' shin bone. No matter how old these bones may or may not be, this whole relic business is new to me. It is not part of my tribe's tradition, which probably explains why I can't get my head around it. I need some fresh air.

On the lawn in front of the chapel a large stone cross dating back to the 18th century casts its shadow over the altar situated in front of it. I pause for a moment in the sunshine at these two symbols of sacrifice and commitment, the altar and the cross. Two thousand years ago Jesus made the ultimate sacrifice on the cross at Calvary and the commitment of his twelve disciples led to the transformation of the world.

Six hundred years later, Columbanus and his twelve companions committed themselves to the way of the cross, offered themselves to God as living sacrifices and in so doing totally changed their society. For me, the cross, in practically any shape of form, has become such a powerful symbol filled with deep meaning. I think this is true for many people. I am continually surprised at the reactions the cross provokes. After my religious conversion as a young man, I began to wear a cross on the lapel of my denim jacket. The very sight of it made one of my friends ask in disgust, "Why are you wearing that *fenian* thing?" Years later, while serving as a pastor in the eastern part of Germany, the sight of the cross on the gable wall of my church one rainy evening, was enough for a suicidal young woman to seek help and find hope. The cross almost always provokes a response.

Today, as I stand at the foot of a weather-beaten cross with its accompanying stone altar, I am once again surprised by the power of the cross. How much am I prepared to sacrifice to change my world? How much am I prepared to die to self? How much I am prepared to lay on the altar? How deeply am I prepared to love, no matter what the cost?

Beyond the altar are the foundations of an eleventh century church and the site where Saint Columbanus built his first monastery when he arrived here around 590. Archaeologists using magnetic resonance techniques have discovered a settlement under the earth in the field adjacent to the church, thought possibly to be the original Columban monastic settlement. I realise I am standing on a site of massive historical significance for European civilization and religion. I am standing at the headquarters of the celtic mission that transformed medieval Europe, the nursery to hundreds of missionary monks who would establish churches and monasteries throughout western Europe.

It is no exaggeration to say that Christianity is the dominant religion in Europe today largely because of the place where I am standing right now. And yet, looking around me, this is not obvious. The place looks so normal, so unimportant—nothing but a little chapel and some old ruins resting in the tranquillity of the French countryside. But this is indeed holy ground. This is what the celtic Christians called a 'thin place', where the distance between heaven and earth is so minimal they are almost touching. God-shaped space. Holy. Special. Blessed. Strange as it may seem to us, the unspectacular, the unassuming, the seemingly insignificant are often signs that the kingdom of heaven is near.

Annegray could also have been known as a thin place to those first monks from Bangor for an entirely different reason. They arrived at Annegray in the autumn and had no time to plant crops or gather food for the winter. Provisions were thin on the ground. Columbanus and his companions often had nothing to eat but wild berries, forest herbs or the bark of young trees. I know I have made some sacrifices as a missionary in Germany, but in light of Columbanus' sufferings they seem frivolous. Although, come to think of it I did once have to drink jaggy-nettle tea whilst visiting one of my church members!

In truth, my needs have always been met. I have always found that God has provided for me just when I needed it. That is why the first verse of Psalm 23 is so special to me: "The Lord is my shepherd. I shall not want." My priorities in life have changed. My wants have changed. I guess I now understand what my mother used to say, "Enough is as good as a feast." It is truly liberating to live by this truth.

Columbanus and his companions would often prove the truth of such words of scripture as they experienced God's providence on numerous occasions. Not long after they were settled in the wilderness of Annegray, an abbot belonging to another monastery was told by God in a vision to send food supplies to the newly arrived Irish monks. When the servant delivering the food could not find his way through the dense forest he let the horses guide him. They led him on an unknown path through the forest directly to the Bangor monks who thanked their Creator for His benevolence. I hope they thanked the horses too.

When word got out about God's miraculous providence for His servants in the wilderness of the Vosges mountains, people began to flock to Annegray. Many of them were sick and infirm, seeking prayer and healing at the hands of the holy man of God from Ireland. Besides healing the sick, there were other wonders attributed to Columbanus, including replenishing the monastery granary, multiplying bread and beer for his monks, breathing on and breaking a cauldron of beer that was a sacrificial offering to a pagan God, and taming a bear and then yoking it to a plough. Incredible. Some things are simply inexplicable.

We make our way back to Jacques' place for some lunch—juicy melon with ham for starters, chicken and some good old *pommes frites* as main course, followed by a selection of cheeses. *Délicieux*. I have always loved the smell of coffee but do not actually like the taste of it, preferring instead to drink tea. In this part of France, however, they seem to be coffee drinkers, so I am now drinking espresso coffee with three sugars after every meal. At least it keeps me alert, which is useful when trying to understand all the French that is going on around me.

Whilst finishing off my espresso with *beaucoup de sucre* I notice Madame Dupont beating through the bushes in the garden, lifting up rhubarb leaves and looking under them. She then makes her way through the vegetable patch doing the same. Curious, I ask Patrick and he informs me she is looking for the tortoises. There are two tortoises which basically are free to roam anywhere they want around the garden. Nice idea, free range tortoises, much tastier than your average tortoise I reckon.

I get up and help her, checking the patio the steps and the area around the house. I mean, how far can a tortoise get? Which leads me to tell my first ever joke in French:

"What did the snail that was riding on the tortoise' back say?"

"Whoaaaa...!"

I think my hosts laugh more out of a mixture of courtesy and pity rather than amusement but I don't mind, I told a joke in French. That may be no big deal to some people, but for me it is, and I am well chuffed with myself. I suppose it is all a matter of perspective, just like the snail riding on the back of the tortoise. To us the tortoise is the epitome of slowness, but for a snail sitting on the back of a tortoise moving at top speed it is definitely a white-knuckle ride.

I intentionally carry this thought about perspectives with me as I spend the next three days sightseeing in Luxeuil. I want to see and consider things from different angles. Whilst firmly rooted in my own tradition, I want to expose myself to new and different perspectives that will hopefully challenge my thinking and prevent it becoming one-dimensional. Little do I realise that, like the snail in the joke, I too would sometimes have to hold on tight and feel like screaming with joy... or fear.

Chapter 13

Site Seeing

Jacques' knowledge and expertise on all things Columbanus are simply staggering. Together with Patrick they really are a dream team and I could not ask for better tour guides. Jacques tells me that Luxeuil-les-Bains, as it is known today, had originally been a small Roman town named Luxovian. As the Roman empire waned, the Romans increasingly under attack from barbarian invaders, were forced to retreat back to Rome. This meant that when the monks arrived from Bangor at the end of the sixth century, there was nothing left of Luxovian except a few old ruins of Roman villas.

Columbanus' monastic settlement nearby at Annegray had grown and expanded to its full capacity. A new site was needed to accommodate the steady influx of students seeking learning and spiritual guidance from the Irish monks. They were granted the old Roman site in Luxeuil, five miles from Annegray, and proceeded to lay the foundations for what was to become the most renowned and prolific of Columbanus' monastic centres.

A few years later a third site at Fontaines would be established and between them they would become the major hub of mission sending missionary monks throughout Europe, including six hundred and twenty missionaries into Bavaria alone. I can't help admiring the incredible pioneering spirit and evangelistic zeal that was so commonplace among them. They don't make them like they used to.

The monks that went out from Luxeuil, Annegray and Fontaines were not only trained in the Holy Scriptures but also in the arts and the sciences, in history, classical literature and in modern and ancient languages. The Bangor missionary monks saw education as a blessing, which explains why they were instructors in every known branch of science and learning of their day. Columbanus could refer with ease to both pagan and Christian authors. For him there was no clear distinction between the sacred and the secular. Everything belongs to God and is of God. One could worship God just as easily working in the field as in the sanctity of a church service. Both are equally valid, and indeed equally important.

This was one of the aspects of celtic monasticism that was so attractive and so different when compared with the monasticism of the Roman church of that day. Roman Christian monasticism tended to lead to a complete withdrawal from society in order to live the holy life untainted by the sinful world outside. Celtic monasticism was different. Columbanus did indeed expect his monks to practise contemplation by withdrawing from everyday life in order to seek God in solitude and prayer. However, he also expected them to then get involved in society and bless it by being a holy transformational presence. That's why the Bangor monks taught their students the things that the celtic seminaries were famous for: holiness, learning and manual skills. I often wonder how things would be if theological seminaries lived this model today.

One of the places Columbanus would withdraw to was a cave on a hill between Luxeuil and Annegray. Here, surrounded by the beauty of nature, he could pray and meditate, undisturbed by the busy demands of life as an abbot. From the vantage point of this hill, Columbanus could also watch over his two monastic centres nearby.

I am delighted when Jacques offers to drive us up to the cave. We squeeze into his little Fiat car and make our way along the narrow road that winds its way up through the forest Saint Maria de Chanois. We arrive at a beautiful viewpoint at a quaint little church, complete with car park. It is not difficult to understand why Columbanus would spend time here. The view is majestic, the nature stunning, the tranquillity therapeutic. I wish I could bottle some of this and take it home with me.

Patrick tells me that the "Friends of Saint Columbanus" look after this site, cutting the grass and maintaining the pilgrims' pathway that leads back down to Luxeuil. They certainly do a good job; the place is immaculate. I then see the familiar bronze plaque tribute to Columbanus that I had seen at Bangor Abbey as I started my Columban journey. It is mounted on a rock at the entrance to the cave where Columbanus is thought to have stayed. The rock floor is larger than the roof, suggesting that the cave was originally bigger. Today it is basically just a niche in the rocks, albeit, as Jacques reminds me, a niche with a history.

Columbanus once encountered a bear in this cave and calmly commanded it to leave. It did so and never returned. Once, when he was on his way through the forest to the cave Columbanus became surrounded by twelve wolves that closed in on him. He froze and quietly prayed to God to protect him. The wolves came right up to him, sniffed at his cloak, then left without harming him.

Another story tells how Domoalis, one of the young Bangor monks who often accompanied Columbanus to the cave, was thirsty and complaining about always having to descend the hill to fetch water. Columbanus reminded Domoalis of how God had provided water for the children of Israel when they were in the desert. He pointed to a spot directly in front of the cave and ordered his young companion to begin digging.

Domoalis obeyed and discovered a water source exactly where Columbanus had ordered him to dig. It is 35 degrees today and I am glad this water source is still available, located just a few yards in front of the cave. Patrick tells me that sometimes pilgrims come here to drink from this water in order to be healed. I sit down on the grass beside the stone trough and drink from its refreshingly cool mountain water. I feel better already.

I follow Jacques and Patrick into the little chapel adjacent to Columbanus' cave. The chapel, which was built in 1872, is only twelve feet wide and eighteen feet long, but its arched windows and elaborate masonry make it look more grand. The little bell tower built onto the front apex of the roof not only gives the building a certain charm, but also highlights its significance as a place of pilgrimage. The chapel is no longer used as a place of worship but rather as a place of prayer for the many visitors and pilgrims coming to see Columbanus' cave.

Inside the chapel the walls are decorated with various photographs and newspaper clippings. There are no pews, just a narrow bench along one side of the church. The main focal point is the marble altar above which stands a large statue of Columbanus, complete with mitre hat, the traditional headwear signifying a bishop or an abbot. Pilgrims often place flowers on the altar as a mark of their respect for the saint. Today, a red rose rests on one of Columbanus' outstretched hands.

A book containing handwritten prayers lies open on the altar. These prayers, written by visitors, are prayers of thanksgiving or prayers asking for help or blessing. Jacques informs me that the book is used often, and normally needs replacing within a year. I browse through some of the prayers written by people from all over the world in all kinds of languages.

As I write my own prayer into the book I sense a oneness with the many strangers who have been here before me. Like them, my prayer asks for God's blessing on my family, my loved ones. People actually want the same thing, no matter where they come from or what language they speak. Why is it always easier to see what divides us rather than what unites us?

Back outside the chapel I spend a few minutes alone sitting on a bench beside a large stone cross, where once a year, on the fourteenth of July, an open air service is held to celebrate Bastille Day, France's day of national celebration. Today all is quiet. I am quiet. Thankful. Pensive. I reflect on the exemplary lives of Columbanus and his twelve Irish companions. Their holiness and devotion to God was so infectious, so attractive that many wanted to know more about their Christian faith. The purity of their lives was indeed one of their primary means of evangelism. Heathens experienced the monks as they truly were, without hypocrisy or self-righteousness. What you see is what you get, and the heathens liked very much what they saw because it was so completely different from the otherwise debauched living that was commonplace at the time. What would Columbanus think if he were around today? I wonder.

No doubt the monks' holy lives were shaped and formed by the disciplined practice of withdrawing from the busyness of life in order to seek prayer and solitude—retreating to places like this, where I am sitting today, in the beauty and stillness of the Vosges mountains. This was however just one factor that helped shape the holiness of the monks, one factor that was part of a larger discipline, the so-called 'Rule of Columbanus'.

In Bangor, Columbanus had known and lived under the strict monastic rule of Colmgall, the abbot of Bangor Abbey. Now an abbot himself, Columbanus introduced an even stricter code of conduct for the monks under his care. The Rule of Columbanus was made up of rules for community living (*Regula Monachorum*) and rules to aid personal holiness of life (*Regula coenobialis*). For a while, the Rule of Columbanus was even more widely practised in Europe than the Rule of Benedict which would however later become the standard in all monasteries on the continent. Under Columbanus' rule, each day had its familiar rhythm of three-hourly blocks devoted to prayer, manual labour, academic studies and devotional reading.

Columbanus considered all sins that threatened or endangered community life to be especially serious. There were harsh punishments for brothers who, through carelessness or lack of consideration for others, disobeyed the rules of the community and threatened its harmony.

Punishment by beating was the norm for any monk who failed to lock the main doors of the monastery at night. Monks who stole were required to do penance for four years, or indeed eight years for the sin of bearing false witness.

It was forbidden for monks to visit the room of another monk or to get undressed in the presence of other monks. Casual conversation with a woman without others being present was also forbidden, as was leaving the monastery without permission. The Columban monks took vows of obedience, poverty, chastity and silence. Their food was basic. Those looking for eternal reward should only satisfy their real needs in this life. And it was considered a grave sin should a monk, who had stuffed himself with food and wine, vomit out the sacramental host (body of Christ) after taking Holy Communion. Columbanus also expected his monks to renounce all worldly goods, avoid vanity, exercise discretion and practise the mortification of the flesh as a means of limiting impure fleshly desires.

Although I acknowledge the value of discipline and sacrifice in living the spiritual life as a follower of Christ, I find a lot of these medieval practices extreme, and indeed bizarre. On the other hand I can't help thinking it would do us all no harm to reconsider our values and priorities in relation to worldly possessions, obedience, faithfulness, serving others, keeping our promises, and living a balanced life of work, study and contemplation. We should however drop the practice of punishment beatings for forgetting to lock the doors at night, or alternatively, install an automated door locking system with key codes, as is the case with the monastery in Luxeuil today. Very humane indeed.

If you have ever wondered where the notion of the confessional box in Catholic churches came from, look no further than Columbanus. Besides the 'Rules', Columbanus also wrote another work during his stay in Luxeuil, entitled *De poenitentiarum*. This work, dealing with penitence, introduced the practice of the confessional into Europe, where sinners would confess to a priest who would in turn stipulate the penitence that was to be done for sins committed. Whilst still very much en vogue in the Roman Catholic church today, the Protestant Reformation of the sixteenth century led to the abolishment of this practice of confession in Protestant churches.

My guided tour continues back in Luxeuil at the basilica of Saint Peter and Paul. This is the magnificent church built on the site of the former Columban monastic churches of the thirteenth and fourteenth centuries. The sun is blazing down on us and I am glad when we get inside the church which is delightfully cool, in both senses of the word. Patrick points out the various historical and architectural highlights of the basilica to me, including the fourteenth century tomb of a knight, the magnificent seventeenth century grand organ and the eighteenth century pulpit which used to be in the cathedral Notre Dame de Paris. We finish our tour of the church at the neo-gothic shrine of Saint Columban's relics.

As soon as we step outside the church we are hit by a wall of stifling heat. It is thirty-five degrees Celsius today but it feels even hotter as the heat unrelentingly radiates off the pale granite paving stones around the church. Jacques is still full of beans, but I am beginning to wilt in the heat, succumbing to the demands of trying to understand everything in French. I am now only managing to grasp a fraction of what is being said, as I constantly seek refuge in every possible piece of shade on offer.

Then Jacques does something that immediately gets my full attention. He invites me to take a step back in time. Over two thousand years back in time. Right outside the basilica there is a fenced-off area around the site of an archaeological dig that has uncovered parts of the Roman settlement that existed before Columbanus' abbey. The crypt of Saint Valbert, the third abbot of Luxeuil, was also found here. Standing looking through the wired fence I am able to see some of the stone sarcophaguses that have been uncovered and date back to the second century. There are one hundred and twenty-five of these ancient stone coffins in total, many of them still in near perfect condition, and most of them without their stone lids. Thankfully they are also without their contents. Now you know why 'sarcophagus' is Greek for 'flesh eater'.

Jacques needs to remove the water that has gathered on the plastic sheeting that acts as a roof covering the site. He opens one of the fence elements to gain access to the site and asks me to accompany him. We move carefully along the planks of wood that are a part of the scaffolding that weaves its way across the site. Jacques and I remove the water from the roof by pushing it to the outer perimeter of the scaffolding where it cascades to the ground well away from the archaeological dig. I follow him through the scaffolded walkways hovering over stone coffins, open graves and other signs of life gone by.

I am surprised by how interesting I find it all. I have never really understood people's fascination with antiques or their interest in historical artifacts. In my ignorance I usually end up telling them that a common rock on the ground is actually much more ancient. But standing in the middle of this archaeological dig, the site of a pre-Christian Roman villa which would later become the foundations for an early medieval Christian church, I begin to understand. I find myself trying to imagine how life was for those who lived and died here all those centuries ago: those who buried their loved ones here; those who worshipped in the church that was built here, before it became covered in a thousand years, and a thousand layers, of dust. I begin to understand what drives people to quite literally dig up the past.

I suppose in some ways it is no different today—if you really want to get to know someone you normally need to dig deeper. Over the past few days I have been able to do just that and get to know amazing people like Jacques Dupont, one of *Les Amis de Saint Columban* in Luxeuil. As we part, I am conscious that my words of gratitude are totally inadequate. I will never forget his infectious enthusiasm and I will always be indebted to him for helping me dis-cover the cradle of the Columban mission in Europe.

Chapter 14

This is my Body

I am wakened early today, not by the sound of doves chanting on the roof, but by the sound of flies buzzing around my window. I get up to investigate and discover that they are not flies at all, but wasps industriously—and irritatingly—coming and going from their nest right outside my window. I have never been stung before and intend to keep it that way.

Closing the window and the wooden curtains, I fall into bed and drift into an uneasy sleep with the faint sound of buzzing wasps in my ears. This obviously plays on my sub-consciousness because in my state of semi-slumber I begin to dream of wasps. My dream however soon turns into a nightmare, in which I am being attacked by a monster wasp that is buzzing around my head.

The dream is so vivid and frightening that it actually startles me out of my sleep. For the next three seconds, in a state of disorientated panic, I fight off my imaginary attacker, until my brain cells gradually become active enough to realise that the buzzing is just the alarm clock of my mobile phone, vibrating on the table beside me.

Deranged chanting monks that turn out to be pigeons, and monster wasps that are nothing more than the wake-up call of an iPhone. Whatever next?!

Today is Sunday and it is living up to its name. A vertical slice of sunlight is able to divide my room in half because the wooden curtains, when closed, only almost touch. A million dust particles, wakened out of their slumber by my frantic efforts to fend off an imaginary monster wasp, float aimlessly in and out of the shaft of light. I sit on the bed and observe them, happy to let their hypnotic motion bring my pulse down to pre-fight-or-flight levels.

Breakfast consists of iced tea and the four croissants I bought yesterday evening at the *boulangerie*. I don't normally eat four croissants for breakfast but Madame Boulangerie threw in two extra for free as it was just before closing time and I was her last customer. My spirits are high, as will my cholesterol levels be.

The socks and jeans that I had washed in the sink last night and hung out over the balcony outside my window are bone dry. Before slipping them on I check carefully that they are wasp-free and remind myself not to panic should my phone happen to 'buzz' in my pocket sometime later today.

I have some time before church so I decide to explore the little town of Luxeuil on my own, taking photos of the main attractions and anything else that catches my eye. Seventy-three photos later I discover the town's cemetery complete with war memorial in honour of those fallen in the First World War.

All around me are white crosses, many of them inscribed with the words, "ICI REPOSE UN SOLDAT INCONNU 1914-1918" (Here lies an unknown soldier). I am reminded of the anti-war song by the Fureys, "Here in this graveyard it's still no-man's land; the countless white crosses stand mute in the sand". I think of the unimaginable suffering, pain and loss that France suffered at the hands of her neighbour, Germany, during two world wars. I then think of how these two countries have been able to heal the wounds of the past and move on to form a strong partnership in Europe today.

This point is driven home to me when I get into a conversation with a gentleman tending a grave nearby. He is from the Alsace, a region of France which has a strong German influence, particularly on the language. I find his Franco-German dialect quite amusing, but this peculiar mix of French and German words actually speaks volumes. If Germany and France can live at peace with each other today, especially given their history, then why shouldn't we be able to do so in Northern Ireland? Then I am reminded of one of the reasons why it is so difficult. Religion.

At its best it is simply irreplaceable. At its worst it's tragic. That's why when Jesus named his followers 'salt of the earth' he was also quick to warn them that salt that has lost its saltiness is useless. Sadly, much religion in Northern Ireland is bad religion; religion that has lost its saltiness. Instead of bringing people together, it divides. Instead of facilitating inclusion, it can be a means of exclusion, where the different religious factions act like door men—or as we say in Belfast 'bouncers'—blocking the entrance to their night club and deciding who is in and who is out. I am about to discover that religion lacking in seasoning is not just confined to Northern Ireland.

As part of my Columban journey, I had thought it would be appropriate to be worshipping in the monastery Church of Saint Peter and Saint Paul today, especially as Patrick is conducting the service. Unfortunately this is not to be.

Patrick has already spoken to me and implied that it would be a problem for him if I came to the Eucharist, as only fully fledged Roman Catholics are allowed to receive Holy Communion in the Catholic church. Sad, even if my own theological understanding of Holy Communion differs from the Catholic understanding.

Being true to myself, and out of respect for the views of others, I would not expect to actually receive communion at a Eucharist service (mass) in a Catholic church. I am nevertheless surprised by my own irritation at my implied exclusion from the worship service itself. I find it ironic that Holy Communion, an act that celebrates Christ's work on the cross, breaking down all barriers and reconciling us to God, has become something that creates barriers and divides Christians. I can't help thinking that the bread and the wine here could do with a wee pinch of salt.

In the Methodist Church any and all who seek God's grace are invited to take part in and receive Holy Communion. We invite people not to a Methodist table but to the table of the Lord. He is the host, and all who sincerely seek Christ and his grace are invited to and welcomed at the sacrament of Holy Communion.

Things being as they are, I will be attending *L'Église Évangélique* today, one of the Protestant churches in Luxeuil-les-Bains. I found out about this church last night from a couple at a table beside me as I enjoyed a cool beer at the unimaginatively named *Café Français*. My new French friends were able to tell me that there are three Protestant churches in the town. The nearest one is known as *Le Temple*, a more traditional church, but there are no services there today so I make my way to the small free-church nearby.

As I enter the church I read the words of Jesus that are found in Matthew's gospel, *"Voici, je suis avec vous jusqu' à la fin du monde."* ... "See, I am with you even unto the end of the world." These words remind me of my own church in Chemnitz which has a similar text on the wall in the foyer, *"Ich will mit dir sein"*... God's words to Moses, "I will be with you". I feel at home already.

I take a seat three rows from the back and survey my surroundings. The sanctuary is typically Protestant free-church and reminds me of some of the gospel halls I know from Northern Ireland—plain, simple, functional. Except for a cast iron mural depicting someone laying down their burden at the cross, there is very little imagery or symbolism to be seen. My time working in the building trade to help finance my studies enables me to identify the *Microlook Dune* suspended ceiling tiles.

Worship is led by an elder, as the pastor is on holiday. There are no hymnbooks. The songs are projected onto a large screen and accompanied not by organ music, but by guitar, electric piano and violin. There are about forty people present with a good mix of age groups. The fellowship seems warm and friendly with many of the church members sharing in conversation with one another before the service begins.

I feel quite relaxed and at home even though this is my first visit in this church. I am a pastor. This is my world. I know how things work in a Sunday worship service; what I am supposed to do and more or less what to expect when I attend church, even if it is a French service I am in today.

Ministering as I do in the atheistic context of eastern Germany I am however also aware that there are many people who have never been in church and have no idea what to expect should they decide to attend a worship service. For many people it can be quite a daunting thing to attend church. They have no idea when to stand or when to sit; the hymns and the liturgy are usually alien to them and they probably don't know anyone in the congregation. I have been a visitor to certain churches where not one person has said a word to me the whole time I was there. Church can unfortunately sometimes be a cold and lonely place for strangers. It's a sin, really.

Thankfully it is not a sin committed in the little *Église Évangélique* in Luxeuil today. I have only been sitting here for about five minutes when I am approached by a lady who greets me with a friendly smile and warm welcome. As it happens Paula is the perfect person to welcome me today. She is English. She introduces me to her husband Matthew who then introduces me to a couple of other folk who speak German, and within a few minutes it is as if I am one of the family. Well, strictly speaking I am actually.

There is something very special about immediately being made to feel welcome. This is what I love about church when it is true to its calling. One love, one body, one family of brothers and sisters. One big bunch of misfits. Strangers and friends. Saints and sinners. I find this so attractive.

I enjoy singing the songs in French but I don't understand very much else of the service, except that is, for the sacrament of Holy Communion. It would be almost impossible for a Christian not to understand this part of the service. The words and the symbols of bread and wine symbolizing the broken body and shed blood of Christ are so simple and yet so profound and meaningful to Christians all over the world. No matter what country you are in, as a Christian you recognize these words, "The body of Christ, given for you—The blood of Christ, shed for you" You may not understand anything else in the service, but Holy Communion you will understand. It overcomes all language barriers and difficulties.

As the elder administers the bread and the wine representing the body and blood of Christ broken and shed for all humankind on the cross, he remains silent. Back in Germany when I administer Holy Communion in my church I normally say, "The body of Christ" as I offer the bread, and "The blood of Christ" when giving the wine. The person receiving the sacrament would normally then reply with "Amen", meaning literally, "Let it be so".

Today however the elements (bread and wine) are administered without words. As I come to receive them I simply say *"Merci"*. It seems appropriate. It feels right. What more can one say, other than a simple thank you? Who can really fully appreciate and understand what is going on when we celebrate Holy Communion? It is for this reason that I encourage children to participate at Holy Communion. I respect some people's argument that children are too young to understand what's going on at Communion. But does anyone really understand? I know I don't. Not really. Not fully. And I'm o.k. with that. The song we sing during Communion underlines Christ's suffering on his blood-soaked way to the cross at Golgatha. Without grumbling and complaining, bruised, bleeding, alone he went:

Il s'avance, Il s'avance vers le Golgatha;
Et le chemin est impregné de son sang.
Sans murmure et sans plainte
Meurtri, sanglant, seul Il va.

Even though I understand the French, I can never fully comprehend what those words actually mean—that God would choose to die for me rather than punish me. All I can do is say a heartfelt *merci* for His mercy. On good days I also live that *merci* out in my life.

After church I am invited to *partage*. This is the monthly church community lunch which—lucky me—is happening today and is being hosted by Paula and Matthew at their place just outside Luxeuil. They have arranged for me to drive there with Nancy, a member of the congregation who lived in Germany for thirty years. We converse in German allowing me to hear more about their church and its dear members who have so welcomed me into their midst today.

Paula and Matthew have a beautiful home hidden deep in the Vosges countryside. They live in what used to be an old primary school that has been tastefully converted into a beautiful guesthouse and *Gîte*. The place is simply oozing character. When we arrive most of the congregation have already sought the coolness of the old assembly hall, its rustic state of repair only adding to its charm. The high ceiling and thick stone walls provide an ideal escape from the midday sun and the clammy heat. Just perfect for the gathering today.

Nancy disappears into the kitchen with her home-made quiche and I take my place at a table near the back of the hall. Opposite me is a middle-aged lady I do not recall seeing at church this morning. Her name is Jenny, a school teacher from England, on holiday with Paula and Matthew for the summer. Pierre, the man who played the guitar at church this morning, sits down beside her and soon all three of us are conversing fluently in *franglais,* a mixture of French and English.

Every so often we have to revert to sign language to make ourselves understood which is no small feat considering the subjects Jenny raises. She has been on a journey of discovery searching for the meaning of life, and so for the next hour we talk philosophy, world religions, contemplative spirituality and quantum physics. (At least I think that is what we talk about!)

Jenny, like many of her contemporaries, seems to be an adherent of religion-to-go, a lighter version of pseudo-Christianity that does not make demands on or complicate the modern day self-serving lifestyle. Throw in a few elements of far eastern religions along with a sprinkling of esoteric what's-in-it-for-me superstition and you end up with the patchwork religion that seems to be so trendy in the fickle minds of many Europeans today. No wonder the apostle Paul talked about the 'scandal of the cross'. The Christian faith, with it's message of peace, meaning and wholeness through a life of love and self-sacrifice, will always be counter-cultural.

The conversation has been fascinating but demanding, and I am relieved when Matthew interrupts and calls us all to lunch. Perhaps Jenny is equally relieved.

The banquet of food on offer at *partage* is extraordinary. Everyone has brought something. Everyone that is, except me, but the church members are quick to welcome me to their table, assuring me that they are delighted to have me as their guest today. The sense of happiness and community created by the genuine warmth and kindheartedness of my new friends is contagious. This is the true Church, the body of Christ. Church is not the buildings but the members. One body, many members, united in and under Christ as the Head.

As I tuck into my barbecued chicken and pasta salad topped with delicious home grown tomatoes I realise again the significance and importance of table fellowship. I reckon if Jenny just opened her eyes here she would not have to look much further to find the meaning of life. Bridges are built when people eat together. Walls that divide are torn down when people share a table and commune with one another. I think this was why Jesus shared his table with all kinds of people. He dined with saints and sinners, prostitutes and preachers. He excluded no one from his table, and I am grateful that this little church has not excluded me from its table today.

A fine selection of cheeses accompanied by rich red wine makes this Holy Communion with my new French brothers and sisters complete. I go in peace, having enjoyed a foretaste of the heavenly banquet prepared for all humankind.

Chapter 15

The Most Embarrassing Moment
of My Life

I wake at 6.30 am and pack the last few things into my rucksack ready for the trek ahead of me today. Sitting on my bed in the stillness I give thanks to God for the time I've had here in Luxeuil. I have been truly blessed.

On my way home from Paula and Matthew's place yesterday I was able to stop and briefly look around the church in Fontaines, the site of the third monastery set up by Columbanus, who spent almost twenty years establishing these monastic communities in and around Luxeuil.

For all the success that Columbanus enjoyed, his time in Luxeuil was not without its difficulties. The Roman bishops were unhappy that the Irish monks acted independently and did not consider themselves to be under their authority. Relationships became even more difficult when Columbanus criticized the bishops for their questionable lifestyle. His uncompromising attitude also got him into trouble when he refused to baptize the bastard children of King Theuderich II of Burgundy.

Theuderich's grandmother, Queen Brunhild, retaliated by scheming to get Columbanus and the Bangor monks expelled from Luxeuil in the year 610. They were sent under escort to Nantes on the Atlantic coast where a boat was supposed to take them back to Ireland. But this was not to be. The boat taking them to Ireland got stuck on a sandbank not far from shore and the crew interpreted this as a sign from God that the monks were not meant to leave France.

The captain of the boat turned back to shore and set the monks free. With the help of Theuderich's half-brother, King Theudebert II, they made their way inland, heading east over Paris and Metz before crossing into to present day Germany at Trier. Following the river Rhine, Columbanus and his compatriots made their way south by boat all the way to Lake Constance. The missionary zeal of the Bangor monks would lead to numerous faith communities being established among the German-speaking peoples in this region which today borders Germany, Austria and Switzerland.

If I am going to have any chance of making it to Columbanus' resting place in Bobbio, Italy, I need to be on the road early today. Unlike the Bangor monks, I have not been expelled from Luxeuil. I do however have an escort for the next part of my journey, but his remit is not to ensure that I board a boat taking me back to Ireland. Instead, Patrick has offered to drive me to Belfort, as I make my way towards the Swiss border and the next stage of my Columban adventure. I hope to get as far as Saint Gallen today, the Swiss town founded and named after Columbanus' right hand man, Saint Gall.

When I go out into the yard, Patrick is already waiting for me at his car, a two year old Nissan Micra. Judging by the number of dents and scratches on the bodywork it is obvious that Patrick also drives like a clergyman. I throw my rucksack into the boot and take my seat in the car hoping that today is a quiet day for guardian angels.

My concerns are unnecessary. Patrick's driving is exemplary and we arrive safely without incident in Belfort. Goodbyes said and promises of postcards exchanged, I shoulder my rucksack and watch Patrick's little red Micra mingle into the sea of traffic heading out of town. I am so grateful that our paths crossed and although we only met a few days ago I count Patrick as a friend. I was a friend in need. He was a friend indeed. A true gentleman and I enjoyed his company immensely.

I walk about three miles with the sun blazing down on me and the sweat almost tripping me. Two lifts later, separated by another three mile hike, a battered black Mercedes stops for me. Thirty-year old Vitaly is from Russia but has been living in France for the past fifteen years. He is unemployed and on his way to a job interview this morning when he picks me up. Thankfully for me the job interview is in St. Louis right on the border to Switzerland. As so often in life, one man's loss is another man's gain.

We share our experiences of living in countries that are not our place of birth—the challenges of learning a new language and adapting to a new culture. Vitally tells me that he could never go back to Russia, as much as he loves his homeland. He has changed so much since arriving in France. He thinks differently. He sees things differently. He is not the person he once was and could never go back to be the person he was in Russia. Changing his environment has changed him. Forever.

Vitaly leaves me at the outskirts of the town, but his words do not. As I walk through the streets of St. Louis towards the French-Swiss border, I mull them over in my mind pondering what they could mean in my case. Will I ever go back home to Northern Ireland? Will I *never* go back home to Northern Ireland? Vitaly is right. Changing your environment does indeed lead to yourself being changed. Having lived almost fifteen years in Germany I know this to be true. I am not the person I was fifteen years ago. Who is? But the thought that I might have changed so much that I will never be able to go back home, is not a pleasant one.

One and half litres of mineral water later, I arrive at the *Landesgrenze*, clearly marked with the Swiss and French flags. I nearly get arrested by Swiss border guards who start screaming at me when I try to take a photo of a border sign showing the flags of the two countries.

It baffles me that you are able to cross the border unhindered—even entering a non-EU country—without having to show any identification at all. But try taking a photo of a street sign, and you could be deported quicker than the time it takes to open all the blades of your Swiss army knife. It makes me wonder why the security checks at airports are so thorough if the border controls on land are so non-existent. Kind of defeats the purpose, me thinks.

Thinking about my near-death encounter with the irate border guards I am wondering if they have informed their counterparts at Interpol who are now following my every move by means of military satellite orbiting the earth. If so, they will now be observing me walk through the Swiss border town of Basel. With the technology at the disposal of the intelligence services today they will probably also be able to notice that I am sweating profusely—due to the thirty-six degree heat, although the proverbial third degree from the border guards is probably also a contributing factor.

I am one of the few pedestrians on the impressive Johanniter bridge crossing the vast river Rhine. I imagine Columbanus and his brothers rowing up the river below me, constantly having to row against the flow, never having the comfort of drifting and allowing the river to carry them forward. To aid them in their efforts Columbanus composed the *carmen navale*, a boat song that speaks of perseverance in hard times and the help that comes from Christ. I decide to do the same, mumbling to myself a little tune I make up in order to lift my spirits. Unlike Columbanus' ditty however, I doubt that my song will still be remembered fourteen hundred years from now, but at least it puts a spring in my step as I cha-cha-cha my way through the streets of Basel.

It takes me some considerable time to get a lift from Basel to Zurich, and it is already early evening when I arrive in the city centre. Realising that I will not reach Sankt Gallen tonight, I decide to look for accommodation here in Zurich. I make myself comfortable in a trendy little internet café and order myself a tea, a piece of carrot cake and one hour's online time.

I send a few requests for accommodation in Zurich over the couch surfing website that I am registered with. It's a long shot, but one that actually works out for me because within ten minutes I get an offer of a couch for the night. Tarzan, my host's screen name, tells me that 'we'—I presume he and his wife—live not far from the city centre. He then emails me his mobile phone number so that I can contact him from the road. I finish my tea, pay my bill and start making my way through the urban jungle that is Zurich to Tarzan and Jane's place.

My prospective host has already texted me his address but I am having difficulty finding it so I text him requesting further information. For the next half hour we converse by texting one another:

"on Breitenstraße now. Which way from here?"

"go 2 end. R onto Gruner Weg then 2nd L - Margaretenstr"

"thx. where 2 now?"

"up hill 2 traffic lights. B4 lights turn L. Klarastr 136 on R"

"thx. c u in 20mins"

Twenty minutes later, I am standing in front of my host's house, a chic apartment complex. I notice the flashy sky blue BMW that is parked in the driveway. I also notice its unusual registration plate, ‚LA-DY 1‘, and am pleased to see that this 'Tarzan' knows how to treat his 'Jane'. I take the lift to the top floor apartment where my sofa for the night awaits. When the doors of the lift open, a well dressed, clean-shaven young man greets me with a friendly smile.

"You must be Tarzan", I joke, holding out my hand to greet him.

He laughs. "Just call me Clemens", he replies as he shows me into a very chic apartment which consists of two floors. The upper floor is open plan, the kitchen being separated from the main living area by a breakfast bar. At the end of the breakfast bar, a square column, obviously some kind of structural support, runs from floor to ceiling.

My hosts have creatively turned it into a focal point in their living room, allowing previous couch surfers to scribble graffiti messages, greetings or pithy words of wisdom all around it. Clemens shows me where the coloured pens are kept and informs me that all guests are expected to sign the wall of fame. Seeing the works of art up there I feel under pressure already.

Tarzan, or rather Clemens, is thirty-two years old and, when not entertaining couch-surfers in his apartment, he works as a chemical engineer for a large pharmaceutical company in Zurich. We sit down at the kitchen table and Clemens offers me a drink. I am so thirsty I just ask for a large glass of tap water. My host takes a pint-sized Guinness glass out of the cupboard and fills it with iced water from the fridge. Perfect. We engage in some small talk... where are you from? What do you do? Really? A pastor? On a pilgrimage? We have never had a pastor stay on our sofa... etc. etc.

Tarzan is easy-going, friendly and hospitable, and I quickly feel relaxed in his company. I remember the "we" from his text messages and am eager to meet `Jane`.

"I take it you don't live here alone, Clemens. Is there a woman in your life who is due home any minute?"

"Oh, no, no. I live here with my brother. He should be home in about twenty minutes after he has closed up the shop."

I had honestly never thought of this eventuality and at first I try not to let my surprise show. My clergyman head had simply taken it for granted that the "we" and "us" in my host's text messages referred to him and his wife. I decide to come clean with my host.

"Oh, for some reason I had presumed you lived here with your wife or girl-friend, but now I see that this beautiful penthouse suite is a bachelor pad for you and your brother", I offer disarmingly.

Clemens smiles. "That's right. It's just the two of us. My brother actually owns the place, along with the beamer downstairs in front of the house."

"His shop is obviously doing pretty well to be driving such a nice car. What line of work is he in?"

"He has his own perfume and make-up shop. He sells beauty products."

As if on cue, the front door opens and a well dressed, clean-shaven, young man enters the apartment. A definite case of *déjà vu*, and for a split second I think it is Tarzan who has just gone out and come back in again. All becomes clear when I am introduced to 'Jane', Clemens' twin brother, Stefan, who welcomes me to his home.

At first glance, Stefan is more or less another Clemens—only one that smells better. Not that Clemens smells bad. It's just that Stefan's clothes have absorbed the perfumed fragrances he has been selling all day in his shop. After shaking Stefan's hand I turn to his brother Clemens.

"He certainly smells better than you, Clemens", I joke, knowing that both brothers would see the funny side.

"Yeah. No one moans when Stefan brings his work home with him", Clemens answers dryly.

"Occupational hazard", Stefan adds, as he pours a glass of milk and joins us at the kitchen table. "You should see the looks I get sometimes when I have to use public transport."

The classy BMW sitting outside the house pops into my mind. "If I had a car like yours I wouldn't be using public transport".

"Yeah. It's a great car. I love it. But my shop isn't far away and it's easier to walk into town". My curiosity gets the better of me. "The number plate is something else. LA-DY 1—did you choose it yourself? And who is the lucky 'lady' in your life that gets to drive it?"

"No, there's no one", Stefan answers as cool as a cucumber. "I just liked this number plate".

If my wife were with me now, she would be discreetly

signaling to me: "Don't go there!" I hesitate, my curiosity almost getting the better of me, but in the end, I listen to my wife's imaginary words and 'don't go there', deciding instead to change the subject. I thank my hosts for offering me their sofa for the night and ask them if they will let me buy them a beer as a token of my appreciation. They like the idea and take me up on my offer. After dinner, we will walk down the road to the little pub on the corner to try out a local brew.

As Clemens puts the last touches to a mixed salad, Stefan fires up the gas BBQ outside on the rooftop patio—a wonderful little oasis overlooking Zürich complete with dining table and matching chairs, various assorted plants and even a potted pear tree. In fact, the only things missing are the three French hens, two turtle doves and a partridge.

The twins, aka Tarzan and Jane, don't need help, so I ask if I can have a quick shower before dinner. Hiking with a heavy rucksack through Zürich in the height of summer has meant my sweat glands have been on overtime.

Clemens leads me downstairs to their bathroom and shows me where to get some fresh towels. I thank him and close the bathroom door behind me as he leaves me to it. For a split second I think of locking it, but I don't. Why should I? My hosts both know I am in the shower. I know that they know I am in the shower. They are trusting me in their home overnight. What would it say if Clemens were to hear me locking the bathroom door behind me as he walks back up the hallway? Don't I trust him? (It doesn't dawn on me to think what it would say if Clemens were to hear me *not* locking the door as he walked away!) In that split second these are the thoughts that cross my warped mind leading me to leave the bathroom door unlocked.

As I get undressed, however, I don't need to think at all. I simply set my brain's autopilot up for the shower routine and it knows exactly what to do.

It knows to get me undressed first and then turn the shower on without getting in until the water has warmed up sufficiently. Of course it knows it would be more efficient to turn the shower on first and let the water warm up while getting undressed. But it also knows it is impossible to do this without getting your sleeve wet. No matter how fast you are, the falling water is usually all over your shirt before you have got your arm out of the way.

Autopilot also knows that the problem would be solved by first undressing the top half of the body before turning on the shower, but it has been programmed by its creator to ignore this option. Autopilot knows all this, and so as usual I find myself standing naked in the bathroom waiting for the water running in the shower to warm up.

It is only when I spot my iPhone that I had placed on the shelf, beside the biggest bottle of *Paco Rabanne* aftershave I have ever seen, that autopilot is disengaged and I take back control of my thinking. Seeing the phone reminds me that I wanted to text my wife, Gill, and let her know where I am. I decide to do it quickly before jumping into the shower. Standing there in nothing but my birthday suit, I reach for my phone and "slide to unlock". It is not just the bathroom door that is now unlocked.

The next five minutes are the longest, and belong to some of the most embarrassing, moments of my life—right up there along with the Sunday I tried to baptize a child without water in the baptismal font, or the time when I was learning German and thought a lady was telling me she was open for prayer when she was actually telling me that my trouser zip was undone. I'm good on embarrassing moments.

When I unlock my phone, the screen opens at text messages, the last app I was using before I put it back in sleep mode to save power. I quickly scan over the page in view and recognize that it is my text conversation with Clemens. I see the text messages we sent each other back and forth as I was being directed to his house. Clemens' text message to me " up hill 2 traffic lights. B4 lights turn L. Klarastr 136 on R", and below it my answer to him "thx. c u in 20mins"

This was the last thing I wrote to Clemens before arriving at his apartment. Or so I thought. Under my last entry to Clemens is another one from me, one that has not yet been sent. This unintentional entry consists of just two characters, 'H' and 'I' but together on the display of my mobile phone they look like the greeting, "HI". I obviously have not switched off my phone properly before slipping it into my pocket, and these two random characters have inadvertently been created by the phone moving about in my pocket before it went into sleep mode.

With the water in the shower still running I go to delete this message so that I can quickly write a new one to Gill. Unfortunately, for some reason unknown to me and about which I definitely want to ask God when I stand before Him on judgement day, I hit the "send" button.

My eyes nearly pop out of my head when I read the word 'sending' on my phone, the little grey status bar increasing in line with my blood pressure. In the five seconds it takes to send the message I am in total panic frantically hitting every possible button and icon on the display in order to cancel sending. Naively, or rather as a confirmation of my total desperation, I even hold the phone under my armpit in the hope that it will negatively affect the signal strength and somehow prevent the message being sent. But it's pointless. "Message sent" appears on the screen of my phone.

A few seconds later, still standing naked on the bathroom floor with the water of the shower running in the background, the electronic beep of an incoming text on Clemens' mobile phone upstairs sounds the death knell for me. Tarzan, and by association his sweet-smelling brother, Jane, have just received a text message saying "Hi", from a stranger in their shower who has intentionally left the bathroom door unlocked. I am doomed.

Chapter 16

The Austrian Mastermind

In the next thirty seconds my mind races. What must he be thinking? He knows I am married... but then again I am traveling alone. We have only just met... but even that means nothing nowadays. He knows I am a clergy man... but... no, I am not even going to go there.

I am jolted out of my irrational mental gymnastics by the sound of an incoming text message on my iPhone. It's from Tarzan. It is the shortest SMS I have ever received.

"?"

Just a question mark, nothing else. As a preacher, pastor and theologian I know how powerful the question mark can be. Jesus was always asking questions. In fact, he had more questions than answers:

"Who do you say that I am?

What will a man give in exchange for his soul?

Do you believe I am able to do this?

Why are you so fearful...you who have no faith?

Do you want to be healed?

What does it profit a man if he gains the whole world and loses his soul?

My God, why have you forsaken me?"

These questions, and loads more. Questions often tell us more than answers ever could. I know all this. I know the power of a question mark. But I never thought I would experience it like this. Not in this context, not in this situation. Not ever. This question mark floors me. I am powerless to think or act in any rational or useful manner. Sweating profusely, I freeze.

Finally, autopilot takes over again forcing me to set my phone down and re-engage my shower routine. I do what I should have done three minutes ago when the world was still very much in order. I get into the shower. Closing my eyes and bowing my head, I allow the streams of water to cascade down over my body as I will them to wash away my wrongdoings.

Only when I am in the shower does it register with me that I have not locked the bathroom door.

This small but significant piece of information causes the status bar of my blood pressure to rise again forcing me to have my quickest shower in living memory. I take even less time to get dried, whistling loudly and nervously whilst getting dressed. Whether the whistling has been a contributing factor or not, I am relieved that the unlocked door has remained shut the whole time, which in effect has been no more than about five or six minutes. Five or six minutes that have put years on me.

Still cringing with embarrassment I consider what my course of action should be when I go back upstairs. How do you explain something like this in a way that both makes sense and is actually credible? What will Clemens and his sweet fragranced brother have thought about such a strange text message from the man in his shower that he has only known for five minutes? Will they have changed their minds about letting me stay overnight?

Still wet behind the ears, I open the bathroom door and make my way up the stairs to the living room where Clemens and Stefan are waiting. I decide that the best plan of action is simply to tell the truth, no matter how ridiculous and incredulous it may seem.

"Clemens, I must apologize to you for the crazy text message you just received from me". Clemens' face is red and he awkwardly looks away revealing just how uncomfortable he feels . "Yes, I wondered what was going on. To be honest, I didn't really know what to think".

I try to explain. "Clemens, I accidentally hit 'send' when I really wanted to hit 'delete'. I actually wanted to send a message to my wife. You just happened to be the last person I had sent a text message to. Your name was still...".

"But Hi?" Clemens is still baffled. "What does Hi mean? Why would you send Hi to your wife?"

"I didn't type 'Hi'. My phone was not turned off properly in my pocket. Those characters were already there when I went to send a text to my wife. But instead of deleting, I hit 'send' by mistake".

Sweet-smelling Stefan, who has been quietly setting the table, bursts out laughing. "I believe you.", he says as he slumps into the chair in stitches. "You couldn't make something that bizarre up. For a minute you had us worried. I mean, who would send a text message from the shower?".

"Yeah, and the "Hi" thing was weird", Clemens adds. "I was wondering if you needed help with the water tap, the hot 1."

Obviously the last ten minutes have been as bizarre for him as they have been for me. "I'm just glad you guys didn't come to investigate whilst I was in the shower."

Over dinner out on the balcony in the shade of the pear tree, the three of us laugh about the whole incident. Clemens tells me they have had many couch surfers staying with them over the past few years but have never experienced anything as strange as tonight. "Yeah, but you've never had a pastor staying with you before", I add, "We are a special breed". Clemens and Stefan laugh. I just stare at my dinner, shaking my head, still somewhat in a state of shock at the weirdness of this whole episode. A smile crosses my face when I think how my daughter Megan is going to give me grief for this. She is always teasing me about how useless I am with my phone. I believe her now.

After dinner, we clear up and walk into town where I buy the guys a beer. I even have one myself. I think after our escapades this evening we certainly deserve it. We enjoy a pleasant evening chatting mostly about work, but also about life and about faith, before heading back to the apartment. Clemens and Stefan have an early start tomorrow so we decide to say our goodbyes tonight. Before heading off to their bedrooms, Stefan reminds me to sign their wall of fame—or in my case their 'wall of shame'—before my departure in the morning.

The twins' bedrooms are downstairs, and I am sleeping in the living room on a corner sofa. Beside me is a mega collection of CDs ranging from Abba to ZZ Top. My corner sofa is mega. When fully opened, it looks more like the kids' padded play area found in some parish halls. I sprawl out in my comfy play pen and let the cool breeze wafting across the rooftops and in through the open patio doors kiss me to sleep.

When I awake at 7am I notice I am about ten feet away from where I went to sleep last night. I always knew that I am prone to twist and turn in bed at nights, but the mega sofa I slept on last night has quite disturbingly demonstrated just how much. If I had slept until 9 o'clock I may well have twisted and turned all the way out onto the roof garden. Thank God it is walled.

Clemens and Stefan have already left for work. I didn't even hear them leave. I sit at the breakfast bar, eating the muesli and fruit they left out for me and wondering what I am going to write on their guest wall. There are messages from all over the world in all kinds of languages. "It would be cool if you could write something in Irish." Stefan's parting words to me last night. I told him that I never had the chance to learn Irish at school—only Catholic children learn Irish in school in Northern Ireland—so English or German would have to do. I pick up the blue marker, find a free space on the column and scribble my greeting which includes practically all the gaelic I know. "The craic was great—sláinte. Barry".

Mission accomplished, I shoulder my rucksack and take the lift to the ground floor. It will be all uphill for the remainder of the day.

Before heading to my final destination in Bobbio Italy, I plan to visit two towns that straddle the Austrian-Swiss border. Bregenz, in Austria and Sankt Gallen, in Switzerland, are sites of considerable importance for the mission of the Bangor monks among the German-speaking peoples of the early seventh century. This is reflected not only in the name of the town Sankt Gallen, named after the Bangor monk Gallus (or Gall), but also in the fact that Bregenz is twinned with the Northern Irish town of Bangor today.

When Columbanus and his compatriots arrived in this region, they set up a monastic community in Bregenz on the shores of Lake Constance. The mission to the German-speaking *Alemannen* was more difficult than among the *Franks* in Luxeuil now that the generous and favourable political support that Columbanus had enjoyed was all but absent. The *Alemannen* also had strong ties to their pagan gods, making conversion difficult. The monks certainly didn't make life any easier for themselves when the bell they used as a call to worship actually scared the birds away, causing tensions with the local huntsmen whose livelihoods were suffering as a result. Sometimes we Christians get grief from our peers, not because we are Christians, but simply because we are idiots.

In Luxeuil in France the mission strategy had been preaching, practising monastic spirituality—along with performing wonders—and educating the population. But among the *Alemannen*, Columbanus and his monks felt the need to demonstrate and emphasize the might and power of God in relation to the other pagan gods worshipped by the germanic people groups.

Columbanus, encountering a group of *Alemannen* worshipping a pagan god, is said to have breathed on a cauldron of beer that was being readied for offering, shattering it to pieces and spilling its contents onto the ground—all four hundred litres of it! Many of those present were so impressed by the power of Columbanus' God that they immediately converted to Christianity. In another incident, Columbanus' right hand man, Gallus, smashed three idols that had been erected in a disused Roman church and were being worshipped there by pagans.

Those methods may have been effective in the Middle Ages, but the Germans I know today would be far from impressed if you even breathed on their beer, never mind spill it all over the floor. Equally, I can't imagine anyone today going into one of the many former churches in Britain that are now a carpet warehouse or some other business and destroying the goods that are worshipped there by shopaholics most Sundays.

As it happens, the initial positive effects resulting from these violent acts to somehow demonstrate superior power carried out by Columbanus and Gallus were short-lived. Some locals reacted negatively to the monks' dealings and tried to make life as difficult as possible for them. The final straw came in 612 AD when two of the Irish monks were attacked and killed in the forest, leading Columbanus to end his mission in Bregenz after only three years.

The fact that King Theudebert II, who had banned Columbanus from Luxeuil, had just defeated Columbanus' current protector in Bregenz, King Theuderich II, was probably another good reason to get out of town quickly.

I seem to be making my way towards Bregenz just as quickly as Columbanus left it. The twins were able to able to link me up with a friend of theirs who commutes to work between Zürich and Sankt Gallen every day. He agrees to take me with him this morning. I will stay the night here in Sankt Gallen, but first I want to spend a few hours in Bregenz, just across the border.

I travel the short distance by train, taking my seat opposite a young lady who is drinking a mineral water. When she lifts her bottle to take a drink I notice the message tastefully tattooed in beautiful handwriting on her forearm.

"There is always hope". What a contrast to the "Fuck the Future" T-shirt I saw a teenager wearing in the train station just a few minutes ago.

Bregenz, lying on the shores of Lake Constance with its magnificent backdrop of mountains is naturally beautiful. I walk along the water's edge and make a mental note to stop here on my way back and take a swim before heading back to Sankt Gallen.

Gallus' church, the aptly named *Galluskirche*, is at the top of a very steep hill. Plodding my way up the hill, I pass a wall plaque demarcating Europe's narrowest house, which is actually not much wider than the plaque itself. I can't help thinking that if all the houses on the hill were as narrow as this one, I wouldn't have so far to walk.

My spirits lift when I arrive at a small drinking fountain in front of a church. They sink again when I realise the building is not Gallus' church, but rather a Capuchin Abbey, home to another religious order within the Roman Catholic church. The Italians named cappuccino coffee after these monks whose distinctive religious dress apparently resembles the caffein drink, or vice versa.

The *Galluskirche* is a little further up the hill, but I decide to stop here at the fountain to take a breather. And a photo. This time I try to get myself in the picture. I set the camera on timer, press the shutter release button and hurry round to pose in front of the fountain. Just as the flash is about to go off a voice from behind interrupts me: "Would you like me to take that for you?" As I turn round to see a young couple walking towards me, the shutter releases taking a perfect picture of a fountain—and the back of my head

"Well, it looks like you are going to have to now", I offer with a smile. They laugh apologetically and I hand my camera to them, showing them how to zoom. "Just don't run away with it", I half-joke, I don't have the energy to run after you".

The young pair have just qualified as physiotherapists. I am tempted to ask them to wait for me at the bottom of the hill to massage my aching muscles.

After my photo-shoot I rest for another few minutes at the fountain. It's only another two hundred meters up the hill to the church, but I can't help thinking that churchgoers here must have the lungs of a Kenyan long distance runner. I fill my bottle with refreshingly cool water before setting out for one final push for the summit. It may only be 500 hundred meters above sea level here, but in this heat it feels more like that zone known to Himalayan mountaineers as the death zone.

The short walk up the street to the *Galluskirche* is nevertheless accomplished without the use of oxygen cylinders, artificial aids or performance enhancing drugs. Finally, having walked in the light long enough today, I enter the church.

I am immediately spellbound by the historical significance of this holy place. It is thought that Roman soldiers where responsible for bringing Christianity to Bregenz, known then as Brigantium, in the first century. They were the first to build a church on this site. When the empire collapsed, the Roman Christians retreated, leaving the church to the pagans who used it for their own brand of worship. In the early seventh century, Columbanus, Gallus and their traveling companions arrived in Bregenz and rededicated the ground as a place of Christian worship. Today, on the site of the original church, stands a fine baroque church, home to a vibrant—and physically fit—congregation of practising Christians.

After looking around the church, I decide to call at the parochial house to see if the priest has a few minutes to spare. I am calling unannounced but that has been the norm on this trip. Why change a winning formula? I ring the doorbell and explain who I am, where I am from, and what I am doing. Being in Austria I can speak German and have no problem communicating. Two minutes later, Pater Bereuter leads me into a reception room and offers me some water mixed with elderberry syrup.

For the next half hour I get to pick Pater Bereuter's brains on my chosen specialized subject: "The life and times of the Bangor Monks in the region around Lake Constance". I quite enjoy being John Humphrys, the quiz master, and Pater Bereuter is definitely 'Mastermind'.

"How did the Bangor monks communicate with the *Allemannen* when they arrived here?"

Pater Bereuter lifts a picture book from his shelf and places it on the table in front of me. "Gallus could speak the language already. He obviously had come into contact with some *Alemannen* whilst at Luxeuil, in France". He opens the book and shows me various paintings of Saint Gallus, some of them still hanging in the church in Sankt Gallen today. I pose the next question.

"In a lot of these pictures there is a bear. What has the bear to do with Gallus?"

The priest flicks a few pages further. "It relates to an episode in the forest where Gallus got a bear to obey him to throw wood on the fire. That's why the bear is the coat of arms of the city of St. Gallen today".

" But Columbanus was the abbot, the leader. Why was the town not named after him?"

The Pater smiles. "Gallus and Columbanus went their separate ways after their stay in Bregenz. When Columbanus and the other monks moved on to Lombardy in Italy, Gallus stayed here in the region"

I had read something of this before setting out on my pilgrimage, but it is fascinating to hear the story from someone as qualified as Pater Bereuther who is from this area. I am glad to let him continue.

"It's not exactly clear why the two friends went their separate ways. Some say Columbanus and Gall had a kind of falling out and Gallus did not want to accompany his abbot to Italy. Others say that Gallus was sick and could not travel, preferring to stay here instead. In any case, it was a problem."

"I don't follow."

"Gallus refused to obey his abbot. Such blatant disobedience was a serious matter and Columbanus reacted angrily, even forbidding Gallus from celebrating mass as long as Columbanus was still alive."

"That's pretty extreme."

"Yes, it was almost like an excommunication for Gallus, especially if he himself understood his sickness to be a sign from God to stay and minister here in this region".

The clock chimes 3 o'clock, but I've started so I'll finish. "How then did the town, Sankt Gallen, come to be named after Gallus?"

"Gallus moved from Bregenz further round the coast

to Arbon, where he had friends who helped him recover. When he had recovered enough, he moved further inland and founded a small monastic settlement. The city of Sankt Gallen grew up around that settlement."

Pater Bereuter is not just a fount of knowledge, but also a genuinely gracious man. He is one of those rare human beings you meet that effortlessly radiates tranquility, peace and a beautiful sense of balance. His manner is endearing and his Christian faith obvious. I thank him for his help and for making time for me today. Before leaving, he gives me a little book about Saint Gallus as a gift. I am doubly grateful when he agrees to sign the inside cover for me. In German he writes, "God bless you on your further journey. Pater Anton Bereuter"

This journey will now take me to the Swiss town named after the Bangor monk who sacrificed everything in order to build God's kingdom in this region—Saint Gallen. But not without first taking that cool dip in Lake Constance that I promised myself.

Chapter 17

The Butterfly Effect, the Grace of God, and Murphy's Law

After my swim, I lie snoozing on the grass in the sun, submitting my aching limbs to some therapeutic heat treatment—as good as any massage if you ask me. Even though I still do not have accommodation organised for tonight, I take my time, enjoying the moment. Supper, cooked on my little camping stove by the shores of Lake Constance, is one of the tastiest ever. The only thing missing is the therapeutic sound of a horse munching grass beside me. Finally, I force myself to make a move. I rinse my pots in the lake, pack everything away and head for the train station.

On the train I use my mobile phone to go online and check out the local Methodist Church in Sankt Gallen. With any luck I might be able to get help there with accommodation for the night. Over the years I have got to know a few of my Methodist colleagues in Switzerland, but not Pastor Peter Gumbal, the minister in Sankt Gallen. I don't even know if he is at home tonight, but there's only one way to find out. I make a note of his telephone number and as soon as the train pulls into the station I give him a call.

I am glad when Peter answers the phone and even more so when he agrees to put me up for the night, albeit on the floor of his study in the church. I don't object, especially considering that Peter himself has just moved into his apartment two days ago to begin his new appointment here. Not having had time yet to unpack and settle in, he is understandably not ready to receive visitors. I am just glad I have a roof over my head for the night, especially at such short notice.

The cool evening air makes the walk up the hill to the Methodist Church a pleasant one. Peter is waiting for me and greets me warmly, before giving me a brief guided tour of his church, which also houses a sheltered dwelling for senior citizens. This would explain why the building has eight floors, three of which are underground. I wasn't aware Switzerland had an underground church.

We go back downstairs to the main foyer and Peter unlocks a door just left of the main entrance to the church. "Welcome to your humble abode", he jokes as he shows me into his office. "I know you have your sleeping bag. I'm just sorry I can't offer you a bed. My apartment is stacked with boxes and furniture that still need unpacked. I hope you don't mind roughing it tonight."

"This is perfect, Peter. I have everything I need. You are a saint for letting me hassle you at all. I am sure you have enough on your plate without me bothering you. I really do appreciate your hospitality, taking in a complete stranger like myself".

"Well now, when I received your phone call I did wonder if you were the real thing. But I checked you out." Noticing my inquisitive look, Peter smiles before continuing. "Before you got here, I googled you... just to check that you really are the Methodist minister you say you are. It turns out you are."

We both laugh. "Good man, Peter. At least you can sleep well tonight. I don't know if I will be able to though", I say with a straight face, then add mischievously, "I haven't been able to check out your credentials yet. For all I know, you could be one of the confused folk from the old people's home upstairs, beginning to dote and not really a pastor at all. Is there a lock on this door?" Once again we both laugh.

After some further chit-chat Peter bids me good night and leaves me to my own devices. I use the sink in the church toilets to wash two T-shirts. I hang them outside over a bush at the front of the church, hoping they will be dry before Peter's pastor colleagues turn up for their meeting early tomorrow morning. It was alright for Moses to experience a burning bush on Mount Horeb, but I don't particularly want my 'drying' bush to be the first thing Peter's colleagues see when they arrive in the morning.

Peter's office, my bedroom for the night, is all I need it to be—spacious. When I move the coffee table to one side, I have more than enough room to unpack my rucksack and roll out my sleeping bag and an air mattress.

The small coffee table is light and easy to move, but before doing so, I am careful to lift the beautiful glass vase, complete with white orchid, and place it out of harm's way high up on a bookcase next to a hardback set of Zürich Bible commentaries. My phone needs charging so I look around for a socket, but the Swiss sockets are different to EU sockets and my plug does not fit. Thankfully, Peter has an Apple Mac computer in his office which I can use to charge up my iPhone by means of the USB cable.

I am sitting at Peter's desk which is situated in one corner of his quite spacious office. About twenty feet away in the opposite corner of the room is the large bookcase on top of which is a row of large Zürich Bible commentaries, standing neatly back-to-back with typical Swiss precision. Complementing the Bible commentaries on top of the book case is the aforementioned exquisite glass vase adorned with the most beautiful white orchid.

I lean over and switch the computer on. What happens next confirms my belief in what is known in chaos theory as the 'Butterfly Effect'. Small variations in the initial condition of a nonlinear system may produce large variations in the long term behaviour of the system, resulting in solutions that are irregular. To put it in layman's terms: a very small incident can begin a chain of events that will have a dramatic impact later on. The popular example quoted is that of a butterfly flapping its wings on one side of the world setting off a chain reaction which eventually leads to a hurricane on the other side of the world.

At almost the exact same moment that I turn the computer on, the last of the Bible commentaries, standing at the end of the row, topples over, knocking against the tall, elegant, orchid-bearing vase next to it. I am twenty feet away behind a desk on the other side of the room, and can only watch in horror as the vase wobbles a couple of times before slowly tipping over the side of the bookcase and crashing to the floor.

Shards of glass explode in all directions, accompanied by a flood of water disproportionate to the size of the vase that had previously contained it. The butterfly effect in action. Or perhaps "Murphy's Law", as we would say in Ireland—if anything can go wrong, it will.

Stepping carefully over the broken glass, I lift the fallen Bible commentary and restore it to its original place at the end of the row. It's only then that I notice that this particular commentary is on "Revelation", the last book of the Bible, also known as "The Apocalypse of John", as it deals with end times. The terrified expression on my face, as I view a dead orchid lying on the stained glass carpet below me, completes the apocalyptic scene for me.

Whatever will Peter think of me? I have just met him, but he is kind enough to let me stay here, and I go and wreck the place. I know that St. Gall smashed a pagan altar in this area some fourteen hundred years ago, but that's a lot different to smashing a beautiful vase that was a gift from the congregation to welcome their new pastor!

In spite of all the excitement, I manage to have a reasonably good night's sleep—on my air mattress and with my shoes and my jacket as a pillow. I knew there was some reason for me bringing this jacket with me. I have been carrying it halfway across the continent and have not yet needed to wear it. It doesn't half make a half decent pillow though.

I wake at 6 a.m. and go outside to fetch my T-shirts from the bushes. They are not quite dry, so I borrow two coat-hangers from the church cloakroom and hang the T-shirts over a radiator. An hour later they are bone dry. I have already packed away my things and am sitting reading when Peter arrives with a nice cup of tea and a roll. The Bible says, "Man shall not live by bread alone, but by God's word." Having already had God's word this morning, I gladly scoff the bread roll, and down my tea.

Peter is incredibly understanding and kind when I tell him about the broken vase. I am sure he is relieved, however, when I shoulder my rucksack and depart, letting normal service resume.

I walk down through the cobbled streets of Sankt Gallen to the *Altstadt*, the old part of town where the amazing UNESCO World Heritage Site is situated, with its wonderful cathedral and world-renowned abbey library. The Protestant Reformed church, St. Laurenzen, is already open and I am eager to have a peek inside.

Typical of many Protestant churches, this one is much less ornate than Roman Catholic counterparts. The pulpit holds a central position in the sanctuary, reflecting the importance of the Word of God in the reformed faith. My entrance is greeted by lively organ music. An organist is practising in the gallery above, his playing aided by a metronome. Listening to the skillfully played music set to the perfect rhythm of the metronome, I envisage God's steady hand on my life helping me to keep in step with the rhythm of His Spirit. I remember how it is when I rush ahead of God's timing and rhythm for my life. More noise than music.

On and around the pillar to my right, a prayer wall has been set up. Whilst Roman Catholics tend to use candles as an aid to prayer, in the reformed tradition many find it helpful to write out their prayer requests and pin them to a cross or a prayer board where others can read them and include them in their own prayers. Alongside prayers written in various foreign languages, there are many in English. I am moved as I read them:

- "Dear God, please let me find true love again. Sarah"
- "Please Jesus, bless my relationship with Peter and help me to better understand his point of view and the difficulties we are having at the moment. Thank you! Penny"

- "Can you please help my husband to find a job. Viola"
- "Dear God, please let my son return safely from Afghanistan. Kathrin"
- "Dear God, please help me to love and accept myself so that I am able to love others with all my heart. Thanks"
- "Please make my parents talk to each other again so that everything will be ok"
- "Dear God, I try to do everything right in my life, but I do so much wrong. Help me to do more good. Thanks."
- "Dear God, show us the way!"
- "Dear God, please help my cat to come back home safely. Monika".

With the organ practice still going on in the background, I take a pew near the altar and pray both for people I know, and also for the people who have taken the time to write their prayer requests on the prayer wall. Will my prayers make a difference? Will they affect the lives of those prayed for, maybe like a spiritual version of the butterfly effect? I believe so. And even if it wouldn't make a difference in other people's lives, it does in mine.

I finish with the Lord's Prayer and then make my way over to the next house of God on my agenda today.

It is still only 7.45 a.m. when I enter the *Stiftstkirche*, the Roman Catholic cathedral built on the site of the old cloister church. Saint Gall is buried in the crypt here which dates back to the ninth century, but a small part of his skull is kept on presentation in the church as a religious relic. The inside of this baroque cathedral is even more impressive than its exterior. I am amazed at the breathtaking beauty and creative architectural brilliance on display in this house of God. No expense has been spared, with gold, silver, bronze, marble and exotic hardwoods all being used to adorn the inside of this magnificent cathedral with altars, angels and sculptures of biblical figures and various other saints. Only in the Vatican itself have I seen anything to rival this.

Coming from the free-church tradition, there is a part of me that thinks that this is all a bit extravagant and unnecessary. Methodist churches are far less elaborate and ornate. Just as I am thinking the money could probably have been better spent on the poor, my knowledge of the Old Testament reminds me of God's instructions to Solomon when he was building the temple in Jerusalem. No expense was spared, with only the best materials sufficing. And when I think of today's modern buildings—owned by banks, oil companies and other multinationals—I am comforted by the fact that medieval cathedrals were built to serve, honour and worship God, rather than mammon.

Looking around, I see that there is only one other person in the cathedral besides me—an old lady sitting down near the front of the church. I take a few moments to explore my surroundings, snapping photos of sculptures, carvings and the magnificent artwork high up on the cathedral ceiling. I sit down on a pew near the middle of the church to be still and pray. Among other prayers, it has been my custom on this trip to pray the Lord's Prayer in all the churches I visit. It's no different here in the *Stiftskirche* Cathedral, "...thy kingdom come, thy will be done, on earth as it is in heaven."

As I silently pray, I am aware that someone else has come into the church. The old man takes a seat near the front. Five minutes later another couple come in, followed by a younger lady who heads straight to the front, lights a candle, prays and then leaves. Over the next fifteen to twenty minutes there is a steady flow of people coming into the cathedral. There are now about fifty of us present, scattered throughout the sanctuary, sitting in silent prayer and contemplation. It is still only 8 a.m. Perhaps this is how the people of Sankt Gallen like to start their day—in silent prayer in the house of God.

Just as I am enjoying this thought, a priest, accompanied by his assistant curate, appears from the recesses of the altar area and proceeds to the altar. As soon as he opens his mouth I realise that the people, including myself, are not all gathered here by chance for early morning prayer before starting the day.

"Welcome to you all, as we celebrate mass today in memory of Saint Rose of Lima".

God in His infinite wisdom, has so ordained it that I am not to finish my pilgrimage in the footsteps of the Bangor monks without experiencing a Roman Catholic Mass. And could there be a more apt place for me than in the cathedral and town named after one of Ulster's finest missionaries? I can't quite believe this is happening.

I think again of the butterfly effect in chaos theory and wonder what series of events could possibly have led to this most irregular solution. As a young teenager when I played the flute in a loyalist marching band, we would deliberately stop outside the local Catholic chapel and provocatively play two or three anti-Catholic songs. After proverbially "kicking the pope" our band would then move on up the road and continue with the parade.

Now, thirty years later, due to the grace of God, the butterfly effect, or Murphy's law (depending on who you talk to), I am in Sankt Gallen, sitting in holy mass in the Roman Catholic cathedral. Certainly a far cry from my teenage years as a member of the Junior Orange Order or a "kick the pope" flute band. I consider getting up and leaving, but I don't want to draw attention to myself, nor disturb the proceedings.

I will not be going forward and actually participating in Holy Communion. But neither am I going to take out my flute and start playing 'The Sash' to wind the 'Fenians' up. Instead, I decide to stay seated where I am and quietly observe all that goes on. And, once I have decided to keep an open mind, I am pleasantly surprised by what I experience at what in one sense could be called my 'First Holy Communion'.

For a start, the first hymn is one which is also in our German Methodist hymn book, which I love to sing, *Wohl denen, die da wandeln vor Gott in Heiligkeit* (Blessed are those who walk before God in holiness). The priest leads the singing *a capella* and, thanks to the wonderful acoustics of the sanctuary, the sound of the congregational singing is amazing. I am surprised that the liturgy is in many ways similar to Protestant worship services, and therefore familiar to me.

The Scripture reading is taken from a passage in John's gospel where Jesus refers to the hypocracy of the religious leaders of his day. They are like white-washed tombs, clean on the outside, but full of dead men's bones on the inside.

There is no sermon or homily, but the words from John's gospel are enough. They speak to me, challenging me to continually review my own life and witness.

Even the remembrance of Saint Rose, in whose name mass is celebrated today, does not bother me as it once would have. I am able to see it simply as a grateful commemoration of a godly woman who lived in the sixteenth century in Peru, and was a blessing to so many of her townsfolk. I imagine it is similar to the way many Protestants remember Luther, Calvin, Spurgeon or Wesley.

When the service ends, the priest and his assistant disappear back into the 'holy of holies' behind the altar. Unlike in my own church, there is no walking down through the church to the main doors for a meet and greet session with the congregation. Instead, there is silence. Complete stillness, as all remain seated. No one is rushing anywhere. All of us sit with the words of the priest ringing in our ears, 'The peace of the Lord be with you.'

Indeed. A peace that passes all understanding. A peace that the world cannot give.

After a while, one by one, people start to leave the cathedral. Silently. Reverently. Some of them kneeling, bowing or genuflecting in respect to their Lord as they go... into the chores and tasks of the new day. Every single one refreshed and strengthened.

Even the one person who didn't go forward to the altar to receive a wafer from the priest.

Chapter 18

Greetings from the Planet Zarg

My body must be functioning like the Swiss rail network, because I wake up at 05.29 am, one minute before my alarm clock is due to go off. I stayed in Sankt Gallen last night, sleeping again on the floor of the pastor's office, although this time thankfully without incident.

The early start is due to the fact that I am running out of time to get my Columban pilgrimage finished. My oldest son, Michael, is starting university in four days time in Northern Ireland and I want to be back in Germany before he flies the nest. Although he has lived most of his life in Germany, I have always been quick to remind him of his Irish roots.

From time to time as my son was growing up, I would recall the 'Lion King' and quote the words of Mufasa, Simba's father, "Remember who you are". Don't forget where you have come from, your Northern Irish roots... George Best, the Titanic, the Giant's Causeway, Joey Dunlop, Snow Patrol, Foy Vance, C.S: Lewis, Van Morrison, Liam Neeson, Kenneth Branagh, Rory McIlroy, Bushmills Whiskey, an Ulster Fry and Tayto cheese and onion crisps.

Michael had planned to study in Germany, but after the numerous 'Lion King' moments in the Sloan household, followed by a gap year working in a voluntary project in

Ireland, my son has now discovered his roots and wants to continue his education at a university in Northern Ireland. When I reminded him that student fees in the U.K. are almost ten times those in Germany, his answer was, "Dad, I've remembered who I am". *Touché!*

This all means I basically have four days to get to Bobbio in Italy, visit the final resting place of Saint Columbanus, and then get myself back to Germany in time to see my son off to uni. For this reason I have decided to use public transport for this last part of the trip. My train leaves at 5.54am.

I change trains in Zürich, having just enough time to buy something for breakfast to take with me on the next train to Milan. There are not many passengers on board and I have no problem finding a window seat with a table. I eat breakfast—the pretzel and bottle of coke just purchased—and sit back and enjoy the ride.

It is nice to be able to sit in silence. When hitchhiking, you are always in a conversation. People want to know about you, hear something of your story, or tell you theirs. This is the 'price' you pay when hitchhiking. But here on this train to Milan, everyone is in their own little world, keeping themselves to themselves. Almost everyone in the carriage is wearing headphones, the most obvious sign in today's society that people don't want to talk, or rather, can't be bothered to. I think 'iPod' is actually quite an apt name for these portable music players. Me, myself, I—alone in my own little pod, cut off from everyone else.

The irony is that, rather than appearing cool and collected wearing trendy headphones, many of these young people from generation 'iPod' actually live incredibly lonely and isolated lives and desperately yearn for meaningful contact, relationship and intimacy. The irony only increases when you realise that the most common electronic device these people plug their headphones into is the very thing that is supposed to enable communication and eradicate isolation. A phone.

But today, on the train from Zürich to Milan, I am happy to be living in 'headphone-world'. I take advantage of the silence around me and gaze out the window as city turns to countryside, to Alps, to paradise.

Although the bright summer sun is shining into my eyes, it would be a sin to pull down the roller blinds and close out such breathtaking beauty: granite walls of mountain rising up beside me; deep ravines filled with green blue water that reminds me of my trip to the Canadian Rockies; stunning waterfalls running into white water rapids where only the rafts are missing; picture postcard farmhouses on the hillside complete with porches decorated with ornamental cowbells and neatly stacked woodpiles; quaint little churches, pretty houses with perfect gardens, and picturesque lakes nestled between majestic snowcapped mountains. On the many occasions that I am in danger of overdosing on natural beauty, the train passes through a tunnel, giving my eyes a chance to recover and ready themselves for the next visual feast.

Having crossed the border into Italy, we stop at Chiasso station, where a number of Italian customs officers, accompanied by armed police, board the train. These *Guardia di Finanza* start checking passports and searching bags. Three of them approach me.

While the first one is checking my passport, the second one is searching my rucksack. He finds nothing but some dirty clothes, a camping stove and a New Testament (I left the Old one at home). Meanwhile the third officer, without saying a word, has handed me a card and is now standing in front of me with a menacing look. I read the text on the card, which is written in English, "Are you carrying more than 10,000 ?" Deciding against making some smart comment, I simply look at the customs officer and shake my head. The whole encounter with the three customs officers takes just five minutes and even less words. Even without headphones.

When I step off the train at Milan central station I am hit by immense heat. The glass roof turns the platform area of the station into a huge greenhouse. Far from cooling me down, the little breeze available feels more like the hot air from a hand-dryer in public toilets. The woman in front of me takes one step off the train onto the platform and vomits. *Benvenuto a Milano!*

I walk to the information desk in the station to enquire about my further route down to Bobbio. There are two long queues but just a fifteen minute wait, made easier by a chat with a young man from Sweden, who has just come from Nice and is making his way to Prague. As you do.

Looking around me I quickly recognize why Milan is one of the fashion capitals of the world. Casual tailoring seems to be the main trend for the men—everything ironed to perfection, but worn casually with rolled-up sleeves, watches that are themselves a fashion statement, and no socks. Standing in the other queue opposite me is one of the most naturally beautiful-looking women I have ever seen. Immaculately dressed, radiant skin and hair to dye for—the sort of person you probably wouldn't expect to find standing in a queue at a train station, unless that is you happen to be in Milan.

The lady at the information desk is seated in a booth behind protective glass. After greeting her with my best *"buon giorno"* I continue in English, bending slightly to speak into the microphone. Her English is good, but the loudspeaker is situated quite low down at about waist level. The general noise of the busy train station makes it impossible to hear her clearly without bending down and putting an ear to the speaker.

Over the next few minutes, as my questions are posed and answered, I am up and down like a yoyo. Bend slightly to speak, bend further to listen, then straighten up to wipe the sweat from your brow in the stifling heat. Anyone watching must think I am doing the actions to the children's rhyme, "Head and Shoulders, Knees and Toes"! My aerobics session finally pays off however, and I leave with all the information I need, including a map of the region and a ticket to Piacenza. From there I will have to find a bus that will take me the last thirty miles further south to Bobbio.

The Trenitalia high-speed train from Milan to Piacenza is most impressive. There is even a full length mirror at every door, enabling passengers to check their style before they disembark. This is Italy. Life is a catwalk.

I exit the station at Piacenza and walk out onto a typical Italien plaza, complete with fountain. To my left is a row of taxis, to my right, a small bus depot. I spot two bus drivers standing in the shade under a tree taking refuge from the heat. I walk over to them and enquire where the bus to Bobbio leaves from. My Italian is practically non-existent, but I am able to ask my question with just one word,

"Bobbio?". I reckon that this, along with raised eyebrows and a gallic shrug, should do the trick.

It doesn't.

The bus driver, who must hold the world record for "most words spoken per minute", explains something to me in Ferarri-style Italian. My puzzled look confirms to him that I am indeed a visitor from the planet *Zarg* and haven't a baldy notion what he is talking about. He consults with his colleague, then calls another one over, who also speaks to me in a *non-Zargian* tongue that I fail to understand. My efforts to communicate in Italian are pathetic—a mixture of French, Spanish, Latin and the occasional English word thrown in with the letter 'o' added on the end, *"Omnibuso Bobbio? Quanta tempus omnibuso? Numero d'omnibuso?..."*

I can see that the three bus drivers are now convinced that I am not an earthling. One of them even squints his eyes and looks up into the sky, obviously looking for the mother ship. But at least these earthlings are friendly, and I am amazed at their patience and eagerness to help. The bus drivers back on my 'planet' would have told me to take a hike by now. This is not so with Piacenza's finest. They persevere until we crack the code.

The breakthrough comes when I realise that Bobbio is not pronounced "Bobby-O", with the emphasis on all three syllabels, which tend to make the town sound like a country and western singer. When Italians speak the name of this town, they say it so fast that it becomes just two syllables, "Bobyo". To include or leave out the tiny letter 'i' may not seem such a big deal, but it is if you're on a tight schedule trying to get to the third major monastic settlement and final resting place of Saint Columbanus.

At least my problems with the letter 'i' are not as devastating as they were at the Council of Nicea in the fourth century, where the inclusion or exclusion of the Greek letter 'i" (iota) in one single word determined whether or not you were a heretic. In fact, Columbanus would play a key role in ridding this region of this heresy, known as Arianism, which was still widely practised in northern Italy in the seventh century.

I finally grasp what the three amigos are trying to tell me. The bus for Bobbio leaves from the bus stop across the street at 3 o'clock. Much ado about nothing. I thank them for their help and bless them with a traditional *Zargian* blessing, before leaving their world, never to meet again.

Seeing the *Banca d'Italia* across the street reminds me that I need to get some cash. I use the *Bancomat* outside, or as we would say in Belfast, "the hole in the wall". The machine seems to be having some problem reading my Zargian card, and decides to keep it, without granting me any money. The only earth money I now have is a fifty Euro note, and I am heading out into unknown territory, just as Columbanus did fourteen hundred years before me. And he had no Euro!

The bus comes spot on 3 pm as promised and I board with the handful of passengers already waiting. The road to Bobbio follows the river that winds its way down through the fertile agricultural land of the Trebbia Valley towards the coastal town of Genova.

It is a pleasant journey, unlike the one Columbanus had to make. When the Irish monks passed through here in the seventh century they would have done so having just crossed the Alps on foot. There were no tunnels, no air-conditioned trains or buses for them. Their ascetic lifestyle also meant that Columbanus and his fellow countrymen refused to travel by horse or cart. Even more amazing when you consider that Columbanus was over seventy years old when he made the journey.

Whilst the journey itself was certainly a difficult one, the conditions awaiting Columbanus in Italy were most favourable. The Lombardian King Agilulph had come to faith through Columbanus' preaching. After his marriage to the Bavarian queen Theodelinde, also a devout Christian, Agilulph set about doing all he could to spread the gospel. For this purpose he gave Columbanus the ruins of a Roman church, along with a tract of land at Bobbio.

Columbanus would only spend one year at Bobbio before his death. But here, on the banks of the river Trebbia, in the year 614 AD, he would establish another major centre of celtic missionary monasticism that would play such a definitive role in shaping the future of Europe. Beside a church dedicated to Saint Peter, arose the walls of an abbey which would incorporate what would become one of the most important libraries in medieval Europe. I can't wait to see this place.

Chapter 19

The Devil's Bridge in a Holy Ghost Town

When in Rome do as the Romans do. Which is why I buy myself an ice cream with two scoops of vanilla and yoghurt, as soon as I get off the bus at Bobbio. I pick up a map of the town and various other info sheets at the little tourist office beside the bus stop. The cheapest accommodation sounds like a palace, but I later discover that the *Ostello di Palazzo* is actually just a hostel near a palace.

Bobbio is a beautiful little town that has kept its medieval character and charm. The expansive plazas and impressive historical churches are linked by narrow cobbled streets, lined with restaurants, shops and cafes. The windows of the stone clad buildings are graced with painted wooden shutters and window boxes decorated with a variety of potted plants and flowers. An impressive fountain dominates the main plaza in the town centre. The town's inhabitants, however, are conspicuous by their absence. Where is everyone?

When I arrive at the hostel, the main door is jarred open. I explore the hallways, the communal kitchen and living room, where I meet a middle-aged Italian couple. They do not speak English. I do not speak Italian. We communicate in French. The couple help me phone the person in charge who arranges to meet me at 6.30pm. This gives me three hours to see some of the sights in town. I thank the Italian couple for their help, leave my rucksack in the corner of the communal living room and head out to explore Bobbio on my 'ownio'.

My first stop is the abbey, a spectacular construction, with its grand multi-arched corridor leading to the Abbey Museum. Here at the *Basilica di San Columbano*, the site of the original abbey built by Columbanus, I enquire if there are any tours planned. Even though the young lady at the information desk is wearing a T-shirt with the words, "Give Love" on it, I am not surprised to discover that she does not speak English. Thankfully, a few *Zargian* moments later, info-desk-lady proves to be as resourceful as she is helpful, phoning someone to help us both out. She speaks in Italian to the person on the phone. I understand nothing except for the first word spoken, *"Pronto"*.

I now know that this is an informal way of greeting in Italian on the phone, but when I first heard it I used to think the caller was in a hurry. So instead of saying, as we would in English, "Let's make this short, I don't have much time", I thought the Italians simply used the word *"Pronto"* to save even more time. It was even more unnerving for me when, a few years ago, I had to make a telephone call to Italy, and the person receiving the call answered, *"Pronto!"*. As if you aren't nervous enough, without the added pressure of having to hurry.

Info-desk-lady has finished speaking. With a pleasant smile she hands me the phone, and the message on her T-shirt comes to life. Although I am not really pushed for time, I take the phone in my hand and say, *"Pronto!"*. Doctor Gian Luigi Bertacci is a tour guide, speaks good English, and doesn't half-know his stuff. I explain to him that I only have 24 hours in Bobbio and am on the last leg of my pilgrimage from Bangor to Bobbio via Luxeuil. He offers to meet me in ten minutes. I don't refuse.

Dr. Bertacci begins at the front of the abbey at the large rock bearing the same plaque of Columbanus that I photographed both in Bangor and in Luxeuil. The plaque, found at all major Columban sites in Europe, is a gift from the organisation, 'The Friends of Saint Columbanus'. The large rock is also a gift. It is actually from Bangor strand in Northern Ireland, a gift to the people of Bobbio from Bangor City Council.

For the next hour and a half I get a whirlwind tour of the abbey including its museum, the original 12th century mosaic floor, the remarkable 15th century wooden choir stalls and various statues and frescos of Saint Columbanus in the church sanctuary. Dr. Bertacci is the perfect gentleman. He is a fount of knowledge but also blessed with the necessary portion of humour that keeps him interesting. I intentionally do not go down into the crypt to see the final resting place of Columbanus. I want to make that the last thing I do tomorrow, a fitting end to not only my stay in Bobbio, but also to my whole Columban pilgrimage.

When I return to the hostel I meet the Italian couple again. We practise our French until the landlady comes to show me my room. I take a dorm style room, with four beds. It's cheaper and the only other guests I've seen in the hostel, already have their rooms so I should have the whole room to myself. The bedroom is plain, but clean and sufficient. After a brief telephone call home, I take a shower and change into a fresh T-shirt and jeans. After almost three weeks on the road this will be my last evening as a Columban pilgrim. There is only one way to celebrate this. Pizza!

The pizzeria I choose also has tables outside in a cosy little enclosed courtyard. Far from spoiling the view, the white vests and sheets hanging from washing lines on the apartment balconies overhead actually add an Italian charm to the setting. My Italian is improving, so I order a *diavolo* and a *media coca*. I reckon asking for the bill will be like extracting teeth, but I don't let it worry me just yet. I have a pizza that needs seeing to.

After a tiramisu dessert, I log onto the wifi with my phone and check out train times back to Germany. A few more families with children have come into the restaurant and it's getting quite noisy. Time for me to leave. Pronto. I manage to pay my bill without *multo problemo*, and walk down to the bus-stop at the main plaza. I am hoping the timetable is on display somewhere, so that I can look up departure times to get me back to the train station at non-*Zarg*-speaking, bankcard-munching Piacenza.

I can't believe how many people are at the fountain. Earlier today this place was like a ghost town, but now at almost 10pm, it's teeming with people. Young, old, families, children. It's almost as if the whole town has come to this meeting point as part of a fire drill, except that everyone has taken time to get all dressed up—or put roller blades on. Then I realise that the people in these parts have a *siesta* in the afternoon. It makes perfect sense. Why come out and wilt in the sun, when you can have a nap then come out much later in the evening when the temperature has cooled own to about 25°C?

I soon find the *fermata*. It hasn't moved since I got off the bus there a few hours ago. I have no problem looking up the bus departure times on the framed *orario* positioned on the signpost for the *fermata*. It looks like I will leave Bobbio tomorrow, shortly after noon. It's been a long day and I am exhausted. It is time to go to 'Bedfordshire'.

I wake at 5.30am, having had quite possibly the worst night's sleep of my life. I had the room to myself and the bed was fine, but the noise outside was ridiculous. It sounded like the Annual General Meeting of the Bobbio Moped and Scooter Association was taking place on the street below my window. They were scooting around until 3am, and then I didn't sleep long before the early morning deliveries by lorry started shortly after five.

I get dressed and walk down to the cathedral where I sit in the stillness, half praying, half asleep. It's not a bad way to start the day, even though there is no mass today for me to attend by accident.

I have breakfast in *Cafe Duomo*, using the free wifi to check some emails. My life in the real world is clamouring for attention, but I ignore it and make my way down to another of Bobbio's famous landmarks, the *Ponte Vecchio*. This old bridge, with its eleven irregular archways that span the river Trebbia, is also known as the devil's bridge. According to legend, the devil built this bridge in one night after making a pact with Columbanus who promised him the soul of the first life to cross the bridge. Columbanus outwitted the devil by sending a dog across the newly built bridge. The townsfolk were delighted, although I'm not sure the medieval animal welfare people were too chuffed.

A visit to the town museum situated in the grounds of the abbey reminds me just how important this Columban monastery was down through the centuries. When Columbanus and his monks settled here in 613 AD, they brought various manuscripts and books with them. This, along with the numerous writings of Columbanus himself, was the beginning of what was to become the most important library in all Italy.

At a time when Greek was almost unknown in western Europe, the Irish monks were among the few who were able to translate the writings of Aristotle and Demosthenes. For centuries industrious monks would copy hundreds of biblical and classical texts, making the abbey's scriptorium famous in the medieval period. Every branch of knowledge, sacred and secular, was represented in the library, resulting in the abbey at Bobbio becoming one of the most influential centres of learning of the day.

There is still one thing to do before I leave Bobbio. I still need to visit the crypt in the basilica where the marble sarcophagus holding Columbanus' remains is situated. Exactly how much of him is actually resting in this 15th century coffin is debatable, given that numerous churches claim to cherish various bones of Columbanus as relics. Nevertheless, this is an important part of my journey.

I am quite moved as I stand quietly in the crypt, the final resting place of this Irish saint who accomplished so much for the kingdom of God in Europe. The sculpted figures on all sides of Columbanus' marble coffin portray decisive chapters in the life of this great man and bear testimony to his accomplishments. Like the monastries Columbanus established, or the prophetic words spoken to bishops, popes and royalty alike; the miracles attributed to him or the sending out of missionary monks to teach, serve and love the world.

I think it fitting to pay my last respects to my fellow countryman by reading his last sermon, which I have as a document on my phone. Comparing life to a roadway, Columbanus talks of the 'end of the way' and of heaven as the 'homeland'. "Let us who are on the way, hasten home; for our whole life is like the journey of a single day." *Columbanus Hibernus* passed into his eternal home on the 23rd November, 615 AD, having lived just one year in Bobbio.

Although I have only spent one night in Bobbio, it is also time for me to hasten home. I hope I make this journey in a single day.

Chapter 20

"Na und?"

The return bus journey back up to Piacenza is uneventful, but I only have five minutes to catch the connecting train. I know I will spend hours on the train today, so I rush into the shop at the train station to buy a sandwich for the journey. As I wait in the queue, a beggar is going around asking people for money. I give him two Euro as I place my order at the counter, a ham ciabatta and a coke. As I pay, the person serving tells me to lift a bottle of coke from the fridge on the way out. I do so, then rush out to the platform where my train has just arrived. It won't be until the train is nearing Munich in Germany that I realise I have left my ham ciabatta lying on the counter in the shop. Obviously that beggar needed it more than me.

The air-conditioning on the train is a gift of God. Unfortunately, His gift does not extend to the other two carriages of our train, where the air-con is broken. This leads to more and more passengers from those carriages moving into ours, making it a tight squeeze. And noisy.

Most of the noise is coming from people using their mobile phones. The train is traveling at full speed and still, all around me, there are *"Prontos"* to be heard. The T-shirt on the young woman seated across the aisle from me says, "I've been waiting for you all my life". She is too busy playing on her phone, and misses me. The call centre feeling is made complete when a Chinese man beside me answers his phone and starts babbling away in Chinese.

You might think it would be impossible to hear anything at all in all this din. But it isn't. Sitting in my mobile call centre, reflecting on my Columban adventure, a still small voice speaks to me. It is the voice of God.

He speaks just two words to me. Two words that he has often reminded me to include as a challenge at the end of many of the sermons I have preached. Two words that make a sermon to be something not just about information, but more importantly about transformation. Two words that make sure that a thought isn't just a thing of the intellect, but something that also touches the heart and moves the hand. Two simple words that actually make all the difference. God speaks these two words to me in German.

"Na und?"

Literally, they mean "And now?", but in the German context they are generally used figuratively to express something more like, "So what!". They can be said as a question, or as a statement. Either way, they provoke. When I preach I often build in a *"Na und?"* section into the conclusion of a sermon. They basically help us focus on our response to what we have heard and experienced, by asking, "So what! What are you going to do about it?"

The *Na und?* section of a sermon pulls no punches: "Alright, you've listened to the sermon, you've heard God's word. So what does it mean to you today in concrete terms? You've sung the hymns, prayed the prayers, experienced the fellowship and felt the hand of God on your life today. That's all well and good, but *na und?* So what! What affect will it have on your life? What difference will it make to how you live? Will you go away thinking differently, acting differently, living differently? Renewed, forgiven, restored, revived, blessed, touched, moved, challenged, more thoughtful, more concerned, more considerate, comforted, encouraged, inspired, strengthened, hopeful? Yes, you've come to church, but so what! Is how you go home from church not just as important as coming to church?"

Even above the noise in my train carriage, I can hear God's provocative *"Na und?"* challenge me. "Alright Barry, you have completed your mission. You made it from Bangor to Bobbio. So what?! You have walked, hitchhiked, traveled hundreds of miles. *Na und?* You have met all kinds of weird and wonderful people and stayed in many different and interesting places. And yes, you have enjoyed the hospitality of foreigners, and been helped and blessed by strangers. And now what? *Na und?* You have taken time out, away from your family, and away from the busyness of everyday life to walk in the footsteps of some 7th century Irish monks. So what now, Barry? What have you learned? How has what you have experienced changed you?"

As I contemplate my Columban adventure and God's *na und* question to me, I am overwhelmed with a sense of gratitude for the grace I have received from the unlikeliest of sources. I am deeply humbled by this experience. Many times I was in need, and each time someone was there to meet that need or help me further. People who had no reason to share anything with me, or do anything for me, were incredibly generous and gracious to me. Many people went out of their way for me, went quite literally the extra mile to accompany me to a more suitable pick up or drop off point when I was hitchhiking. I will never forget this.

I will allow this experience to shape my future deeds and willingness to put myself out for others.

And on every part of the journey strangers became friends. Catholic friends. By no means a given among the Protestant working class who grew up during the 'Troubles' in Northern Ireland. As a child, I thought like a child. I thought to be Protestant was to be British. The violent campaign of the anti-British IRA just reinforced my identity as a British Protestant. It was the paramilitary campaign of the IRA that led my father to become a member of a loyalist paramilitary organisation called the Ulster Defense Association (UDA), whose stated aim was to defend the union with Britain. Maybe that's why, for me as a young boy, to be Protestant was to paint the lampposts on my street red, white and blue and to fly the British Union Flag every July to commemorate the victory of the Protestant King William over the Catholic King James in 1690.

To be Protestant was to belong to a particular tribe and let yourself be shaped and formed by the narratives of that tribe. These narratives, reinforced by the terrorists who sought to bomb us into a united Ireland, led me wrongly to view Catholics as the enemy. For me, to be Protestant was to be anti-Catholic. To stop in front of the Catholic chapel and play triumphalist, sectarian tunes with the marching band. To accompany my father to the UDA social club as an eight year old, and sense his pride when he prompted me to sing the loyalist songs I knew by heart, 'The Orange and Blue', 'The Sash' or 'The Green Grassy Slopes of the Boyne'.

To be Protestant was to travel once a week up to 'Long Kesh' prison as a ten year old to visit my father, who had become a so-called 'Loyalist Prisoner of War'. To hang up on my bedroom wall the hand-painted cotton handkerchiefs he sent to me from prison, with their paramilitary emblems and symbols. To graffiti my school bag and playground walls with the red hand of Ulster, complete with the British crown above and the letters, 'UDA', below.

This was the Protestantism of my childhood—a far cry from the expression of true Christian faith and identity in Christ I was later to discover. My new found Catholic friends, encountered on my Columban travels, remind me how far I have travelled. By the grace of God I am not the person I once was. The Protestant faith I adhere to today is more spiritual, more biblical, more true, when compared with the pseudo-political counterfeit of the days of my childhood. My Catholic friends are a confirmation of this.

I am so deep in thought, that I scarcely notice our train has already crossed into Austria, with Innsbruck being the next scheduled stop. God's *na und?* question about lessons learned on my Columban pilgrimage is still occupying me.

I would say I have learned to trust God more. In all circumstances. Nothing focuses the life of faith more than need. In my need, time and time again, God did not disappoint—even when things didn't turn out as I expected or wished. He was my shepherd. I did not want. The periods of time spent alone, whether walking the streets and roads or sitting in the tranquility of a church sanctuary, helped me sense God's presence closer to me. And I've had some great conversations with the 'Big Man' too. As always, he often speaks in and through the unlikeliest of characters and circumstances. And more often than not, his words can be summed up quite simply, yet profoundly, by, "Don't be afraid. Follow me. Let's do life together."

The history of the celtic mission to Europe has also been a fascinating aspect of my trip, and one which has taught me much. The stories of Columbanus, Gall and the other missionary monks from Bangor have left a mark on me. I know they lived in a different era, and I know their understanding of the Christian faith and how it is practised, differs at various points with mine. But I have nothing but the utmost respect for these men of God who heard the call to follow Christ 'even unto the end of the world'. I admire their dedication, their faith, their intellect and the way they integrated their faith into everyday life. For them, there was no sacred and secular, for all was holy, if submitted to God.

My Columban adventure has convinced me more than ever that modern day Europe needs this kind of church. A church that is faithful in calling disciples of Christ who will make the world a better place. A church that is prepared to die to itself in order to serve the so-called "last, lost and least". A church that is more a movement, than a monument—always reforming, and breaking down walls, crossing borders as it reaches out to others in love.

One final thought goes through my mind as I consider God's 'Na und?' to me. Columbanus was over seventy years old when he started building a monastery in Bobbio. He had just walked over two hundred miles from the shores of Lake Constance down to the Trebbia Valley, crossing the Alps on foot in doing so. He had already established influential abbeys at numerous other sites in Europe. There was every reason for him to take things easy as a pensioner, to settle down and pass the baton onto someone else. No one would have thought any less of him; he had already accomplished so much. And yet, at over seventy years of age, Columbanus begins a new venture—in a new country, with a new language, and a new mission.

In fact, it is only as I am thinking about this that I realise how old Columbanus actually was when he left Ireland. Columbanus only set out from Bangor to begin his mission on continental Europe when he was fifty years old. At fifty he was not thinking of settling down and making himself comfortable with a cosy teaching post in the confines of Bangor Abbey. Far from it. At fifty years old Columbanus was about to begin the biggest adventure of his life. In his fifties and sixties he would plant churches, build abbeys, start new projects in different countries and sow the seeds that would re-unite Europe under Christ. If Columbanus is anything to go by, seeing seventy as the new sixty is not a modern thing at all!

My journey has also helped me see life itself as a kind of pilgrimage, with its ups and downs, its adventures and the characters who make life so much more interesting and livable. We all are on a journey in which we all need each other. Or as a certain U.S. pop group would sing, "One tribe, y'all". If only we could comprehend this!

As I travel back to Germany to a new job waiting for me in the German United Methodist Church, these are some of the thoughts that occupy my mind. My new role will involve acting as a bridge builder, sowing seeds into people's hearts. Like Columbanus and the Bangor monks, I will be on the road a lot. I will be involved in starting new projects and planting new churches. One part of the job will involve me working occasionally in different European countries, so I may even have to learn a new language or two. A whole new chapter is beginning in my life, with fresh challenges and exciting times ahead. I will leave the congregations I have served for the past thirteen years to begin a completely new adventure.

In many ways I find this new task daunting. The person who did the job before me was a massive character in the church. It will not be easy to fill his shoes. And do I really want to swap the comfort zone of all that is familiar and safe for a new chapter full of unknowns and potential risk? At my age? After all, I'll soon be touching fifty!

I can imagine Saint Columbanus looking down from heaven and smiling wryly, as God answers my question. God's words, spoken to me in German, are as inspiring as they are comforting. *"Na und,* Barry?" So what!